ALFA ROMEO

© Piagraph Limited and G. T. Foulis & Company Limited 1975
First published by Ballantine Books Inc., of New York in 1971 in paperback
This hard cover edition was made in England in 1975 by
J. H. Haynes & Co. Ltd. of Sparkford for the publishers
G. T. FOULIS & COMPANY LIMITED
Sparkford, Yeovil, Somerset BA22 7JJ

ISBN 0 85429 198 9

Contents

Photographs and illustrations for this book have been selected from the following archives: Montagu Motor Museum, Louis Klemantaski, TASO Mathieson, Old Motor Magazine, The Autocar, George Monkhouse, Alfa Romeo, Ronald Barker, Kenneth Green, David Yelverton and from *Le Alfa Romeo dal 1910* by Luigi Fusi

'Always an Alfa man'

The author of this book, Peter Hull, is well qualified to write about the history – and present-day activity – of the Milanese firm of Alfa Romeo. His knowledge of the technical as well as historical facts that make up the life of the firm cannot be doubted, in the light of previous books he has written on the subject.

I believe that Alfa Romeo have an appeal that is unique and lasting and the slogan 'once an Alfa man, always an Alfa man' has proved true of many of the firm's employees, myself included. My own association with Alfa Romeo dates from 1928 when I was still a university student at the Polytechnic in my home town, Milan. That same year, my mother bought me an Alfa Romeo single-ohc 1500 cc. chassis. I fitted it with four bucket seats and drove it to success – first place in my class in the Tunis-Tripoli High Speed Rally. Then in 1930 I became the proud owner of a 1500 cc. 6-cylinder supercharged Alfa Romeo fitted with a special streamlined body built by Campari and Sorniotti. My taste for racing grew steadily during the early thirties and I became associated with an Alfa Romeo agency selling cars in Milan. In two years I drove Alfas in fifty-eight events, scoring twenty class wins and several 'places'.

In 1932 I left competition driving to graduate to faster machinery, including single seaters. It was then that I began to regret that I had turned down an opportunity to drive an Alfa Romeo 1500 cc. for the newly formed Scuderia Ferrari firm in the famous 'Mille Miglia' race. I had refused for personal reasons which, very soon afterwards, appeared futile and I regret to this day the lost chance of trying my hand in this famous race for the 'Prancing Horse' team. However, in later years, I entered for no less than nine 'Mille Miglia' races and completed seven with three class wins and three second places – all in Alfa Romeos.

The war temporarily put an end to my racing career, but I went back to it as soon as peace returned and in 1948 I won the Tour of Umbria in a 6-cylinder 2500 cc. Touring Alfa Romeo Sedan lent by the factory. This was the last year in which I was actively involved in racing for Alfas. My association with the firm as a driver had lasted twenty years, surely the most unforgettable ones of my life.

But my interest in the firm has survived the years. I can no longer race, but I still buy Alfas for my private use. Apart from owning a 1300 Giulia Sprint, I also have a large collection of vintage cars which for the most part are Alfas. Among my collection is a delightful and immaculate 6-cylinder 1500 cc. supercharged Zagato Special Spider that was delivered in the autumn of 1928 to the famous racing driver, Gaspare Bona of Turin. The car is still in active service and has won many firsts in vintage car competitions all over Europe. I once owned a four seater 6-cylinder RL Normal open tourer; this was sold to make room for a more interesting 6-cylinder RLSS tourer that I dearly loved, but which was eventually sacrificed to the most coveted car of all: the unique and formidable Alfa Romeo RLTF which is the pride of my collection and which is discussed in this book. I shall never part with this car. At the moment I am busy restoring it to its original condition.

A couple of months ago I was in Pontresina, the Swiss mountain resort, when I came across a 1927 6-cylinder two seater convertible. There are very few of these cars left in Europe and the find was a very lucky one. It is now an important contribution to my Alfa Romeo stable which now includes three immensely valuable veteran cars that are an endless source of pleasure to me. The Giulia Sprint waits to be changed for something more modern, but I would never consider trading it in for anything but an Alfa Romeo. I can be certain that whatever model I choose, it will not lack that personal touch and 'breeding' that are the hallmarks of all Alfas. The new car will be the twenty-first Alfa in my possession in forty-two years.

If I have overstressed my own part in the history of the Alfa Romeo firm, it has been to illustrate the truth of the dictum 'once an Alfa man, always an Alfa man'. My age prevents me from active racing, but my enthusiasm has not waned. The powerful rumble of my 1924 Targa Florio racer, and the whine of my supercharged 1500 cc. sports racer of 1928 are living memories of an unforgettable past. It is for this reason that I have been delighted to write this foreword to Peter Hull's book: in so doing I have been carried far back into a world filled with adventure – a world in which the Alfa Romeo saga was and still is a prominent factor.

Count Johnny Lurani

ALFA 1910-1915

By the end of the first decade of this century, Turin, capital city of Piedmont, had established itself as the centre of the Italian motor industry. Then, as now, the main manufacturer in Turin was Fiat, who had won the three major motor races, the French Grand Prix, the Kaiserpreis and the Targa Florio – as well as world wide recognition – in 1907, but there were other Torinese firms that had made or were about to make their names such as Lancia, Itala, Aquila-Italiana, Rapid, SPA (Societa Piemontese Automobili) and SCAT (Societa Ceirano Automobili Torino).

By contrast the other main industrial city of the north, Milan, capital city of Lombardy, could only boast two manufacturers of any note. Bianchi and Isotta-Fraschini. Züst had a branch in Milan making machine tools and hydro-electric equipment, but their cars were built at Brescia, and of the third motor works situated at Portello, then out in the country but today forming part of the north western area of the city, perhaps the least said the better.

This business, known as Soc Anon Italiana Darracq, had originally been established at Naples in 1906 but moved to its new factory at Portello at the end of that year. It was not really a factory but an assembly plant for French Darracq cars. Unfortunately it was not a very successful assembly plant, for two reasons. Firstly the quality of the material sent from the main Darracq factory at Suresnes was often inferior, and secondly the little single and twin cylinder Darracqs assembled at Portello were unsuitable for Italian conditions, lacking both engine power and efficient brakes for the mountainous roads.

The richer Italians who could afford to do so preferred to buy their Darracqs from the French factory at Suresnes, so it is hardly surprising that by 1909 the Darracq works at Portello were facing closure.

Geometra Cav Guiseppe Merosi, the first Alfa and Alfa Romeo designer

8

At that time local Italian labour was used at Portello mainly under the direction of French engineers, but the managing director was an Italian named Cav Ugo Stella. If only the finance could be arranged, here was a golden opportunity to take over the works from Darracq and build a wholly Italian car in Milan which was designed for Italian conditions. Some Milanese business men, who were also motoring enthusiasts, managed to raise a loan, liquidated Darracq, and started the Lombardy Car Manufacturing Co., more often known by its initials as ALFA (Societa Anonima Lombarda Fabbrica Automobili).

The lessons learned from the Darracq failure showed that in order to succeed the new cars from Portello must be robust and up to date in design with powerful engines and good brakes, suitable not only for touring but capable also of taking part in sporting activities in order to spread the name of the new marque.

Ugo Stella did not have to look very far to find a man capable of designing such a car. His name was Giuseppe Merosi, then chief designer for Bianchi, a marque with a fine reputation for touring cars, though which differed from most of its Italian rivals in abstaining from regular sporting activities. However, Stella knew that back in 1904 Merosi had spent a year in Fiat's racing car design department in Turin.

Thirty - seven year old Giuseppe Merosi was not a native of Milan or Turin, having been born in 1872 in Piacenza, some forty miles to the south east of Milan. In the days when there was no car industry he had studied to be a building surveyor at the Piacenza institute, then, after doing his military service, had been one of the founders in 1893 of the Piacenza cycle firm of Ing Bassi & Merosi. By 1898, at the age of 26, he was working for Orio & Marchand of Piacenza and until 1904 he designed Marchand cars and motorcycles which the firm produced in small quantities. From 1904 until 1905 he spent a year at Fiat's and then went to Messrs Lentz in Milan for whom he designed a car, only three of which were built. From the autumn of 1906 until September, 1909, he was with Bianchi.

After leaving Bianchi, Merosi immediately set to work to design the new car for Alfa. This was the 24hp, a very different proposition from the Darracqs, with a four cylinder 4,084cc engine and capable of over sixty miles per hour. Although incorporating no mechanical novelties, the car was very up to date in design at the time, with a monobloc engine, high tension magneto ignition, light alloy crankcase, 3-bearing crankshaft, pressure lubrication, side valves and a fixed head and transmission by shaft enclosed in a torque tube The power output was 42bhp at 2,400rpm and in torpedo or open tourer form the car weighed 1,000kgs, or about a ton, being typically Edwardian in its light construction. An open tourer of the post war period would probably weigh half as much again due to its heavier construction and extra equipment in the form of starter motor, front wheel brakes and so on.

By 1st January 1910, the French personnel from Darracq had left the Portello works, and the now completely Italian staff commenced the manufacture of the 24hp, although it was not until the following June that the name of the firm was officially changed. A most impressive radiator badge was designed for the new cars, confirming the Milanese pride in the founders of the firm, for it incorporated the red cross and the snake, symbols in the emblems both of the City of Milan and of the Visconti family, who were the Dukes of Milan in medieval times. The cross commemorated the part the Lombards, many of them from Milan, played in the Crusades to the Holy Land, led by Giovanni of Rho in 1096. The snake symbolised either the one in the legend according to which Ottone Visconti killed a Saracen on whose shield was depicted a snake devouring a man, or the Longobard

tradition that a snake conferred protection and strength.

A dark blue border round the edge of the circular badge bore the words 'ALFA' at the top and 'MILANO' at the bottom in brass lettering. After 1912 the lettering was changed to white enamel.

In appearance the 24hp was a handsome car and an intriguing photograph appeared on the cover of the first sales brochure issued in 1910. This showed a 24hp torpedo, with a neatly folded hood but without a windscreen, absolutely crammed with Alfa staff, whose status is denoted by their headgear. Firmly on the side of the artisans and engineers is Merosi at the wheel wearing a cloth cap, and beside him is one of the testers, Parmeggiani, also cloth capped. Sales representative Maggioni wears a trilby as does works manager Agostini, whilst chief accountant Zampori affects a bowler, the choice also of one of his underlings, little Maumary, a clerk who looks rather squashed in one corner

The first Alfa car – a 1910 24hp Torpedo as pictured in the first sales brochure, with Merosi at the wheel accompanied by various factory personnel

of the back seat. The best hat of the lot is worn by the only lady, Signorina Di Simoni, Secretary to the Board of Directors, a Raj turban-like affair, with a feather sticking straight up in the air in defiance of the breeze created by Merosi on whom the security of all the hats must have entirely depended.

The 24hp was soon joined by another model on the production line, the 12hp, which was by way of being a smaller version with an 80 x 120mm 2,413cc engine, producing 22bhp at 2,100rpm. The top speed was about 55mph. Like the 24hp, the 12hp was available with open or closed bodywork, but it differed from the bigger car by having three-quarter elliptic springing at the rear instead of half elliptic.

In 1910 the total Alfa production was

11

Competition 24hp of 1912 with Baldoni at the wheel

ten of each chassis type, stepped up to forty in 1911, so that one-hundred cars were produced altogether during the first two years.

It was the smaller model which was the first Alfa to take part in a competition, a regularity rally at Modena in April, 1911. Out of nineteen entries, the doorless four seater 12hp Alfa tourer was one of the six cars to finish without penalty after covering 950 miles in five stages.

.On 14th May 1911 two racing 24hp Alfas ran in the Targa Florio, that fantastic race over the wild, twisting mountain roads of Siciliy, first held in 1906. The Madonie circuit was over ninety miles long, starting from sea level and reaching a maximum height of over 3,500 feet, and the doyen of motoring correspondents, W F Bradley, had described how the scenery could be wild, sun-kissed, flower-bedecked or snow-capped, depending on the altitude. At the lower levels there were irregular patches of green, varying from the lighter green of an English meadow to the dark green of the Italian olive groves, relieved by patches of bright yellow gorse and mauve clusters of clover. There were cacti and eucalyptus trees by the side of the road, gardens filled with roses and geraniums, and fields full of artichokes. At the starting line the stands were bedecked with oranges and lemons. In contrast, up in the mountains there was bare rock, hewn into for the building of villages which seemed to hang perilously on ledges. The very names of the villages themselves are romance to the followers of motor racing – Cerda, Caltavuturo, Castellana, Petralia, Collesano and Campofelice.

From the beginning the Targa Florio had been almost completely dominated by the Piedmontese cars from Turin – an Itala won in 1906, a Fiat in 1907, an SPA in 1909. Only in 1908 had they been beaten by a Milanese car, when Trucco won in an Isotta Fraschini. In

12

1910 a forgotten make from Lombardy, a Franco, had won the Targa Florio, though actually beaten by a little French Peugeot taking part in a race for voiturettes run concurrently.

In 1911 the Targa Florio had lost some of its former glories (happily soon to be revived), and there were only fourteen entries, including the two 24hp Alfas of Nino Franchini and Ronzoni. Conditions were very bad as the cars were sent off from the start at the usual three minute intervals, and we are told Franchini led on the first two laps of the three lap 277 mile race until he retired blinded by the mud thrown up from his wheels. Ronzoni also retired and the race was won by one of the Ceirano brothers, virtually founders of the motor industry in Turin, driving a SCAT, and he was followed home by a Lancia, a Mercedes, another SCAT and a Ford.

Only the two 24hp Alfa racing cars were built in 1911, really differing very little from the standard cars except in appearance. Normally they had two seater bodies – though sometimes a third seat was placed centrally at the back – with simply a bolster shaped petrol tank behind the seats and spare wheels strapped on behind, nearly horizontally in the two seater but vertically if there was a third seat. The sketchy bodywork made their dry weight over two hundredweight lighter than the standard cars, and their wheelbase was nearly a foot shorter. The bolster tank held 28½ gallons to the 15½ gallons on the standard chassis, and the racing cars had steel spoked wheels, whereas on the touring cars these were of wood. The engines on the competition cars were virtually unaltered from the standard ones mechanically, with the same 4.15 to 1 compression ratio, but gave a fraction

A series C 15–20hp model Alfa of 1913, with racing bodywork

more power at higher revs, 45bhp at 2,400rpm, and the maximum speed of the cars was about 70mph.

The name 'ALFA' was painted on the cars wherever possible for publicity purposes in large letters, along the sides of the bonnet, on the sides of the petrol tanks, on the radiator honeycomb, sometimes none too neatly.

In 1912 the 12hp was produced in Series B form and was renamed the 15hp, now producing 25bhp at 2,400rpm, with a maximum speed of nearly 60mph. Production was double that of the 24hp, also now called Series B, one hundred cars to only fifty of the bigger type.

Some improvements were made to the performance of the 24hp in 1913 so that the Series C cars gave 45bhp at 2,400rpm, the same as the 1911 racing cars, and the maximum speed went up to over 65mph. The 15hp cars were given another 3bhp and renamed 15/20hp, progress being shown by the fact that their maximum speed was now the same as that of the original Series A 24hp cars in 1910. Production figures for 1913 were 103 of the Series C 24hp chassis and 100 of the 15–20hp type. These cars had a slightly wider track than the earlier models.

This year saw the introduction of a new model, and the most exciting Alfa up to that time, the Series F 40/60hp. It was felt that something faster than the 24hp was needed for racing, and this was brought about by putting a new engine of over 6 litres into the 24hp chassis and fitting a higher back axle ratio. The chassis otherwise was unchanged. Two racing cars with spider bodywork – two seats and a bolster tank – were laid down in 1913, and then twenty five chassis built in 1914, with less highly tuned engines, were sold to the public for fitting with either four seater or two seater open bodies.

The new engine was of interesting design, with four 110 x 160mm cylinders, giving a capacity of 6,082cc, being cast in two blocks of two with non-detachable hemispherical cylinder heads and overhead valves operated

via pushrods by two camshafts in the crankcase.

There was nothing new in having one camshaft in the crankcase operating the exhaust valves and another operating the inlet valves on opposite sides of the cylinders as this was the basis of all T-head side-valve engines, which were very popular up to that time. The better known L-head side-valve arrangement, with only one camshaft in the crankcase operating both exhaust and inlet valves in a row to one side of the cylinders eventually replaced the T-head arrangement as it could not only be made efficient, but was obviously cheaper to manufacture.

Up to 1913, however, there had been few cars sold to the public with the same overhead valve operation arrangement that Merosi adopted for the 40/60hp Alfa. The arrangement itself was not new, probably the first time it came to notice being in 1904, when the Belgian Pipe concern introduced it on their racing cars in the

14

The 1914 twin overhead camshaft Grand Prix Alfa with designer Merosi at the wheel

Kaiserpreis race as well as on their production cars, and then in 1905 Fiat commenced using it on their racing cars instead of the previous inlet-over-exhaust system they had borrowed from Mercedes. It will not go unnoticed that it was in this 1904/5 period that Merosi himself was working in the Fiat racing car design department.

As has already been mentioned, 1907 was a great year in racing for Fiat, and the Kaiserpreis race, over a twisting circuit in the Taunus mountains, was won by Nazzaro's two camshaft pushrod Fiat with Hautvast's two camshaft pushrod Pipe second. In his account of this race in his classic book 'A Record of Motor Racing, 1894–1908' Gerald Rose wrote 'Both the Pipe and Fiat engines had pocketless hemispherical combustion heads, and this fact probably had considerable bearing upon their superiority in speed.'

Perhaps it should be mentioned that at the time the 40/60hp Alfa came on the market overhead valves tended to be associated more with racing than touring cars as they had a reputation for noisiness. The well known English motoring historian, Michael Sedgwick, has pointed out that although Mercedes were in production with an overhead valve touring car – the '28/95' – in 1914, Fiat preferred side-valves in their touring cars right into the Vintage era, and the first series-production Fiat with overhead valves was the big Tipo 519 of 1923.

The two camshaft pushrod overhead valve design had a famous revival in 1926, when Percy Riley adopted it for the Riley Nine engine in England, and in racing the system more than vindicated itself not only on Rileys, but on ERAs and Connaughts as well, and on road cars it was probably only killed off by the British Motor Corporation on their Rileys in the later 'fifties on economic grounds in the cause of rationalisation.

It must be admitted that on the 40/60 Alfa Merosi did not make full use of certain advantages of the system as exploited by Fiat, Pipe and Riley. On the Fiat the valves were set at an included angle of 60 degrees to each other in the head, but on the 40/60 the valves were vertical in 'the head which was therefore not entirely 'pocketless', though the pockets were not nearly so evident as those on a side-valve cylinder head, so giving a more unrestricted gas flow. Secondly, in the vintage and later designs following on from Percy Riley, the camshafts were placed very high in the crankshaft, well above the level of the base of the cylinders in order to make the push-rods very short and the reciprocating parts of the valve gear as light as possible, so that many advantages of a twin overhead camshaft design were obtained with smaller manufacturing costs. Valve angle of the ERAs of the 'thirties and the Connaughts of the early 'fifties, incidentally, was 90 degrees. On the 40/60 Alfa, as in side-valve designs, the camshafts were simply placed at the top of the crank-case, just below the cylinder block, so long pushrods were employed in view of the 160mm stroke.

Be this as it may, first bench tests of the 40/60hp engine showed it to be highly efficient by the standards of the time, with a considerably reduced fuel consumption compared with other engines of similar capacity. Road tests were also satisfactory, over 75mph being obtained from a chassis fitted with two bucket seats.

The dry weight of the touring version was nearly 26¾cwt, but on the racing two seater this was brought down to just over 23cwt. The production engine had a single carburettor and a com-pression ratio of 4.35 to 1 and gave 70bhp at 2,200rpm, with a quoted maximum speed of just under 80mph.

The racing cars had twin carburettors

and ultimately a 5.5 to 1 compression ratio. Pre-war they produced 73bhp at 2,000rpm, and post-war the power output was increased to 82bhp at 2,400rpm when the maximum speed was between 90 and 95mph.

The first success attained by the 40/60 in 1913 was at the first Parma-Berceto hill climb ever held. This was no typical English hill climb, lasting one minute or less, but a timed journey from Parma, in the Po valley, to Berceto, in the foothills of the Appenines, over a distance of no less than 33 miles. This is over four times as long as the American 'Climb to the Clouds' at Mount Washington, New Hampshire, and getting on for three times as long as the famous Pike's Peak hill climb at Colorado Springs, though much less strenuous as regards gradient.

In 1913 Nino Franchini's 40/60 Alfa came second overall to an Aquila-Italiana ('Italian Eagle') driven by Marsaglia, with Negri's Itala third, Franchini also winning his class in which another 40/60 came second. It is of interest that in the French Grand Prix at Lyons the following year, a team of three Aquila-Italianas was entered with six cylinder engines incorporating inclined valves operated by two cam-shafts in the crankcase via short pushrods tucked in between the cylin-ders. Only one car started and, as Kent Karslake noted in his 'History of the French Grand Prix', the design was evidently so fluid that the car which started had its inlet and exhaust valves on the opposite sides to those that didn't. Sad to say, the car that started, driven by Meo Costantini (later a well known Bugatti driver), covered only one lap before retiring, and that at a speed of 45mph compared with the record of close on 70mph.

In 1914 Nino Franchini and a driver called Giuseppe Campari, who was destined to figure very prominently in the Alfa Romeo story, came third and fourth respectively in the 277-mile Florio Cup race over three laps of the big Madoni circuit in Sicily, behind Felice Nazzaro's and Ceirano's SCAT,

10352

whilst at the Parma-Berceto hill climb Franchini was third behind Costantini's Aquila-Italiana and a De Vecchi, a short lived Milanese make driven by Ugo Sivocci, also destined to make a name with Alfa Romeo.

1914 saw some redesigning of the old 24hp, which re-emerged with the new name of the 20/30hp and a considerably quieter engine after a silent chain had replaced the former timing gears at the front of the engine. Power went up another 4bhp in this Series E model and it is possible that the 20/30 cross-flow cylinder head, with the

Franchini in his 40/60hp Alfa at the 1913 Parma-Poggio-Berceto hill climb in which he finished second overall and won his class

exhaust and inlet manifolds on opposite sides instead of on the same side as in the previous series, dates from the Series E. On the other hand, in view of the spectacular increase in power from the engine obtained after the war, the new head may not have been incorporated until then. The first 20/30 had a respectable top speed of over 70mph.

In 1913 Alfa took the bold decision to

17

1911 12hp chassis

enter Grand Prix racing under the 4½ litre formula due to come into force in 1914. The chassis used was the old 24hp/40/60hp one, with the wheelbase shortened to 9ft 10ins, about 3ins more than that of the 24hp racing cars of 1911. Gearbox and back axle ratios were the same as those on the 24hp and 20/30hp.

The big feature of interest in the new car was the engine, the design of which commenced by Merosi in October 1913, and in February 1914 it was being tried out on the test bench. The first road test, with the usual two seater bolster tank bodywork, was carried out early in May, and the car was reckoned to be ready to race by the end of July. The French Grand Prix at Lyons had taken place by this time, but Campari was entered to drive a GP Alfa (only one car was built) in the 1914 Circuit of Brescia race. In the eliminating trials he covered a flying kilometre at 91½mph, but the race was never held, presumably because of the advent of the Great War. The car was locked away in a pharmaceutical products factory until the return of peace.

The Grand Prix Alfa deserves its

special niche in history, as it seems to have been the first Italian car to be built with a twin overhead camshaft engine. In view of the devotion in future years by Alfa Romeo to this type of unit, this seems only appropriate.

In 1912 Henri, Zuccarelli, Goux and Boillot in France had produced the first twin overhead camshaft engine in the world for the Peugeot racing department, and it was so successful that it was soon copied by various manufacturers in their racing cars including Delage, Sunbeam, Vauxhall, Humber and Straker-Squire, some copies being more slavish than others.

Merosi's design was very up to date with its clerestory or pent roof shaped cylinder head, four valves per cylinder and dry sump lubrication. It was ahead of its time with a valve angle of 90 degrees, whereas 60 degrees was universal in the 1914 Grand Prix, angles of 90 or 100 degrees only coming in after the war in order to accommodate larger valves, when two valves per cylinder were employed. Strangely enough, the first traceable Grand Prix car to employ four valves per cylinder at an angle of 90 degrees after the 1914 Alfa was the 3 litre 470bhp 8CTF Maserati of 1938, better known as the

20/30hp chassis

A 1914 40/60hp with streamlined bodywork by Castagna

two times winner at Indianapolis driven by Wilbur Shaw. Though because of circumstances not a Grand Prix car, the 1922 TT Vauxhall with its very advanced twin overhead camshaft engine designed by Ricardo also had this valve set-up.

The Alfa engine was a four cylinder cast iron monobloc with an integral head. Bore and stroke were 100 x 143mm, 4,492cc; far more nearly 'square' dimensions than any other 1914 Grand Prix engine save the Vauxhall, which was 101 x 140mm. All the other Grand Prix engines were long-stroke, with one exception, the single overhead camshaft two valves per cylinder Fiat. That had dimensions of 100 x 143mm, though whether any deductions should be drawn from this is open to argument.

On the Alfa the valves were operated direct by the camshafts and not through rockers as, for instance, on the twin overhead camshaft Vauxhall, and two sparking plugs per cylinder were featured, where Peugeot and other twin ohc designs only fitted one. Almost certainly the two plugs on the Alfa were more of a 'fail-safe' arrangement than an attempt at increasing combustion efficiency. As on all pre-

Above: The remarkable twin overhead camshaft engine of the 1914 GP Alfa, probably the first of its type in Italy
Below: The 40/60hp push-rod overhead valve engine

vious Alfas, a three bearing crankshaft was employed, but there were two vertical carburettors. More than one carburettor was the exception rather than the rule on 1914 GP engines.

Whether all Merosi's ingenuity and enterprise would have paid off in the 1914 French GP had the car been ready for it is very much open to doubt. We are told that in 1914 his engine produced 88bhp at 2,950rpm, when the single ohc engine of the winning Mercedes in the race was credited with 115bhp at 2,800rpm. Peugeot gave 110bhp at 2,600rpm and 112bhp at 2,800rpm, Sunbeam 108bhp at 2,800rpm and Vauxhall a staggering 130bhp at 3,300rpm, though their engines did not run properly until after the war. The Sunbeam engines had twin carburettors.

As for maximum speeds, that of the Mercedes is given as 112mph, the Peugeot as 116mph and the Vauxhall as 115mph. The Alfas, we are told, did just under 95mph.

Despite his 90 degree valve angle, the diameter of Merosi's valves was quite small, 35mm for both inlet and exhaust, whereas the Sunbeams, a close copy of the Peugeot with a 60 degree valve angle, had 46mm diameter valves. The compression ratio on the Alfa, incidentally, was 5.55 to 1, compared with 5.27 to 1 on the Sunbeam.

Some development work went into the GP Alfa after the war, particularly to the valve gear and head, and when it was raced in 1921 the valve diameter had been increased to 42mm and the power had gone up to 102bhp at 3,000rpm.

The car's big drawback was its use of an old-fashioned chassis, dictated, no doubt, by economics. Although the all-up weight was probably not a great deal more than that of contemporary GP cars, it was certainly a more massive car – longer, higher and with a bigger frontal area and its artillery wheels added to its 1910 look. In other more advanced 1914 GP cars, seat height had been reduced by double drop side rails and, with their wire wheels,

the cars looked smaller, lower and narrower than the Alfa, with much better wind-cheating abilities. In such a contemporary modern racing chassis, Merosi's comparatively short stroke engine would have lent itself to this treatment, epitomised particularly by the 1914 GP Fiats, which were like the GP cars of the early 'twenties in appearance.

To return to more mundane matters, production figures at the Alfa factory had shown an encouraging increase since 1910, when only 20 chassis were produced. The figures were 80 chassis in 1911, 150 in 1912, 205 in 1913 and 272 in 1914. 310 chassis were built in 1915, of which 105 were stored away for sale after the war. The total figures for the different models were 585 of the 24hp and 20/30 type, 320 of the 12hp, 15hp and 15/20hp type, and 27 of the 40/60hp. To which must be added, of course, the one Grand Prix car.

At the outbreak of war the firm employed a staff of about 300 in the factory and office. The Darracq label still seemed to stick to the Alfa, at any rate in England, where they were sometimes referred to in the motoring press as Alfa-Darracqs. It seems possible that the sales of the cars were still continued through the former Darracq outlets, which might account for this, and certainly a few cars were sold in England.

In evaluating the Alfa cars, it can only be said that the proof of the pudding is in the eating, and with only two Edwardian designed Alfas still in existence very few people today have had experience of driving them. One of these cars, a 1910 24hp tourer, is in the Alfa Romeo museum and, strangely enough, bears the London registration number of LK 5304.

Certain writers have described Merosi's Alfa designs variously as 'dull', 'stodgy' and even 'insipid'. They may have been, compared with the supercharged Alfa Romeos of later years, but not in comparison with contemporary designs.

ALFA ROMEO

At the time when Giuseppe Merosi was engaged in designing motor-cycles and cars for Orio & Marchand in Piacenza, another young man four years his junior was graduating in civil engineering at the Naples Polytechnic, some 350 miles to the south. His name was Nicola Romeo, and he had been born in 1876 at a place near Naples called San Antimo. His parents, who were not rich, had made some sacrifices to send him to the Polytechnic, and after his graduation he went to Belgium and obtained a degree in electrical engineering at Liege. To gain experience he spent the next eighteen months working in Germany and France, as well as Belgium.

As well as having technical ability, young Romeo also had good commercial sense, and in 1902 he started a business in Milan after obtaining the agency for American Ingersoll-Rand mining equipment.

This was so successful that in 1911 he was able to found a firm in Milan called Accomandita Ingegner Nicola Romeo & Co to make mining machinery on his own account, with works at 10 Via Ruggero di Lauria. One of his products, a portable compressed air plant called 'The Little Italian' was immensely successful through being supplied to the Army in 1915. It is recorded that so rapid was the expansion of his firm as a result of this, that the number of his employees rose from 100 to 1,200 between June and September 1915 alone.

In the meantime the Alfa works at Portello had also secured war contracts and in 1915 Merosi had designed a generating plant for Army use incorporating the 15/20hp engine. Cars had still been the main output at Portello during that year, but all car production ceased in December when Nicola Romeo bought out the firm from the shareholders. This seems to show that the small firm hadn't exactly money to spare during its formative years.

In January 1916, Romeo was employing no less than 2,500 workers.

In this year Merosi designed a

Giulio Ramponi with a 1913 40/60hp at a race in 1919

compressor for military use called a C-type, evidently a sort of 'Bigger Italian' with four cylinders, two for the compressor and two for the engine which drove it.

As the war continued, there was virtually no stopping a man with Romeo's abilities, and he bought up three small firms at Portello just as he had done with Alfa (calling them Trieste, Trento and Gorizia, names which commemorate the three 'Italian' towns still at the time under Austrian domination) and became head of a big engineering combine. Alfa also expanded, of course, not only in the number of workpeople employed, but also in equipment. Stessano electrical furnaces were installed, for instance, for use in the manufacture of V6 Isotta-Fraschini aero engines under government contracts. Compressors, tractors, ploughs, air brakes, railway equipment – all sorts of engineering products were now being manufactured at Portello.

In February 1918 the name of the firm was no longer Alfa, but Societa Anonima Italiana Ing. Nicola Romeo & Co, and in June 1918 Romeo added three manufacturers of railway equipment to his combine, Merosi actually being manager of a railway works in Naples between 1917 and 1918.

All these changes might well have spelled the end of Alfa car making activities and the extinction of the name, except for one thing – industrialist Nicola Romeo happened to be a motoring enthusiast, and was determined to build a prestige Italian motor car in Milan. He decided to add his own name to the old established one of Alfa, and the result was the extraordinarily mellifluous and romantic name of Alfa Romeo, which was given to all the cars coming from the Portello works after the Great War, and appeared on the radiator badge in place of the single word 'Alfa'.

Production of new cars did not start

until 1921. Before then the ten Series C 15/20hp and the ninety five Series E 20/30hp chassis which had been laid down in 1915 were sold.

A start was made in competitions in 1919, using pre-war Alfa cars under the new name of Alfa Romeo. Their debut was in the 1919 Targa Florio in which twenty five cars started and only eight finished, three 40/60 Alfa Romeos unfortunately being amongst the seventeen non-finishers. Drivers were Franchini, Campari and Fracassi.

At the 1919 Parma-Berceto hill climb, Franchini was third in the 4½ litre class and fourth overall in the Grand Prix car behind Ascari (1914 GP Fiat), Antonacci (Aquila) and Clerici (Bugatti). Franchini did not drive for Alfa Romeo after 1919, but his name should be noted as he was Alfa's original racing driver before the war. Little is known about him except in connection with a short and rather inglorious (not to say expensive) foray into motor racing which Bianchi made with their 'over-square' 145 x 121mm four cylinder cars in 1907 and 1908, at a time when Merosi was chief of their design office. In the 1907 Kaiserpreis Tommasselli and Carlo Maserati had been their drivers, but one of the drivers of the three Bianchis entered in the 1908 Targa Bologna at Brescia was Nino Franchini, so it seems possible Merosi himself had invited him to drive for Alfa some three years later.

The first entirely new Alfa Romeo design after the war, known as the G1 (Series G being a follow-on from the pre-war Series F 40/60hp) was not a success. The decision had been made to build a big luxury car in the medium price bracket, and American methods of design and manufacture were looked at, even to the extent of bringing a Pierce-Arrow car over to Portello for examination.

Pierce-Arrow's most famous car at that time was the Model 66, a huge car with a six cylinder engine of over 12 litres, though not producing much more than 100bhp, incorporating four side valves per cylinder in a T-head. Apart from also having a six cylinder engine

and a not dissimilar appearance as regards the radiator of the prototype, the G1 does not appear to have borrowed very much from Pierce-Arrow design.

The G1 engine was straightforward and conventional with a 98 x 140mm bore and stroke and a capacity of 6,330cc. Its modest output for the capacity was 70bhp at 2,100rpm, using a 4.6 to 1 compression ratio. It was an L-head side-valve, with cylinders in two blocks of three, and non-detachable heads.

A seven bearing crankshaft was fitted, off-set from the centre line of the cylinders, doubtless with the idea of reducing thrust losses on the pistons, and scoops were provided on the big ends to dip into troughs in the sump providing splash lubrication to augment the pressure system. The method of cooling the sump came in for some criticism by the British magazine Automobile Engineer', as it consisted of three air holes running longitudinally through it, which, stated 'Automobile Engineer', would be easily clogged with mud. Perhaps like certain racing Bugattis, which used the same system, the G1 was not supposed to be driven over muddy roads.

All previous Alfa models had had multiple disc dry clutches, apart from the first ten 12hp cars in 1910, which were fitted with the cone type. The G1 clutch had five plates, the two inner ones being lined with Ferodo. The four speed gearbox was separate from the engine, as on previous Alfas, but the G1 was the first Alfa without a torque tube, a triangular torque arm being provided attached at the forward end to a link hanging from a cross-member. The large transmission brake was one of the external contracting type.

An endearing feature of Merosi's designs was his habit of incorporating little unexpected surprises. It will be remembered that on the 12hp model in 1910, instead of fitting semi-elliptic

Giuseppe Campari in his racing 40/60hp in its 1920 form

The G1 Alfa Romeo chassis with twin cantilever rear springs and 6 cylinder side valve engine

springing at the back he had fitted three-quarter elliptics. On the G1 he opted for the unusual arrangement of twin cantilever springs at the rear. Single cantilever springs were popular on luxury cars, giving a good ride; double ones were known to have been used by Unic. Later they were also used on the big 24 litre Napier Lion aero-engined car used by John Cobb at Brooklands track in the 'thirties, which had to cope with some pretty alarming bumps at speeds around the 140mph mark. A feature of cantilever rear springs was that they cut down rear axle unsprung weight but they did not give very felicitous handling on high performance cars, such as the 1925 3 litre Sunbeam or the 1914 GP Vauxhall.

In pointing out that the G1 design throughout was commendable, sturdy construction being the characteristic, 'Automobile Engineer' also noted that it departed from typical Italian practice 'that is to say that accessibility has not been sacrificed in an endeavour to obtain an ultra-clean outline, and apparent simplicity has not been attained by ingeniously hiding parts. On the contrary, ease of inspection, dismantling for repairs or replacement has obviously been given due consideration in the design of the chassis throughout.'

The French engineer and front-wheel-drive expert, J A Gregoire, once wrote that he considered that an engine in which the manifolds are hidden in the cylinder head, the wiring is concealed in covers, and the accessories lurk under the crankcase, all for the sake of beauty, is less good-looking than a motor where the manifolds are clearly seen and checkable and where the wiring, accessories and apparatus are accurately located and accessible.

Sober limousine bodywork on 1921 20/30hp ES Sport Alfa Romeo chassis

Merosi must have pleased both schools of thought with the G1 engine which, with its long ribbed exhaust manifold, was quite handsome in appearance. One other unusual feature on the G1 compared with other Alfa Romeos was the fitting of a 'reversed Elliott' front axle, on which the trackrod is in front of the axle beam instead of behind it. Wooden artillery wheels were fitted as standard.

It was no fault of Merosi's that the car was not a success. The fact is that the tax on big cars in Italy and the high cost of fuel made it uneconomic in the market for which it was designed. After two prototypes were built in 1920, a small series of only fifty chassis was laid down in 1921/22, several of which were sold in Australia, where one is still in existence today. A further batch of G2 cars, with a reduced bore of 98mm which was planned for production in 1923 was subsequently cancelled. The two prototype G2s gained first class awards in the Garda Cup

rally in December, 1920.

Concurrent with the G1 was a really successful model, known as the 20/30hp ES Sport, produced in 1921 and 1922. This was a development of the original 24hp, and shows how basically sound that old design must have been. Although the only obvious change to the engine from that of the Series E 20/30hp was an increase in the bore from 100mm to 102mm, bringing the capacity up to 4,250cc, the big increase in the power obtained from 49bhp at 2,500rpm

20/30hp ES Sport Torpedo, with Vittorio Rosa at the wheel

to 67bhp at 2,600rpm indicates that the redesigned cylinder head with different porting may date from 1921 rather than 1914. Electric lighting and starting was now available, wire wheels with knock-on hubs could be had as an extra, and the wheelbase was shortened to make it identical with that of the 1911 racing 24hp, 9ft 6ins. With open bodywork the ES Sport was capable of over 80mph.

29

RACING WITH THE OLD DESIGNS

In the winter of 1917, twenty year old Enzo Ferrari was out of a job, and sat disconsolately on a bench in the snow in the Valentino Park in Turin. His father, who had run a small engineering works making equipment for the State Railways in his hometown of Modena, had died of pneumonia in 1916, and so had his elder brother, Alfredo. Called up in the army in 1917, Enzo served in the 3rd Mountain Artillery, where, in view of his metalworking background, he was given the task of shoeing mules. After a few months he fell quite seriously ill, and when he was finally discharged from the army he tried to get a job at Fiat, but there were no vacancies.

Finally that winter he did manage to land himself a job in Turin, working for a man who bought secondhand light truck chassis, overhauled them, and then had them fitted with open sporting bodywork in Milan. This was quite a profitable business in those days when there was a shortage of cars. Young Ferrari's job was to test the chassis, and often to deliver and fetch them from the Milan coachbuilder.

Whenever he was in Milan he always called in at the Bar Vittorio Emanuele, where he became very friendly with Ugo Sivocci, a thin balding man who had driven a De Vecchi in competitions before the war, coming sixth in the 1913 Targa Florio, and had just retired from the sport of bicycle racing.

At that time Sivocci was chief tester at Costruzione Meccaniche Nazionali in the Via Vallazze, makers of the CMN car, which featured new chassis fitted with war surplus 4CF Isotta-Fraschini engines. He persuaded Ferrari to join him there, so Ferrari made the move from Turin to Milan.

It was with CMN that Ferrari had the opportunity to fulfill one of his three boyhood ambitions – to be an opera singer, a sports writer or a racing driver. There were no openings at the CMN works for opera singers, nor was there a demand for sports writers, but there were opportunities for racing drivers, and Ferrari took part in his first event in 1919, the Parma-Berceto hill climb, at the wheel of a CMN, and came fourth in the 3 litre class.

Ferrari's autobiography 'The Enzo

Testing racing ES Sport chassis with Ramponi driving

Left to right, Sivocci and Ferrari in ES Sports and Campari in his 40/60hp before the 1921 Targa Florio

Ferrari Memoirs' (Hamish Hamilton, 1963) is full of good stories concerning his expedition to take part in the 1919 Targa Florio, when he and Sivocci drove the length of Italy from Milan to Sicily in the CMN they were to drive in the race. Whilst going through the Abruzzi mountains in a blizzard, they were chased by wolves, which Ferrari shot at with a revolver he kept under the seat cushion.

In the race itself, when they had been driving for some nine hours and, due to the petrol tank coming adrift, were some one and a half hours behind the winner – Andre Boillot's Peugeot, which had already crossed the line – they entered the village of Campofelice with one or two other stragglers in the race. To their surprise three 'carabinieri' stood in the road and motioned them to stop.

The 'carabinieri' explained that there had not been an accident, but the President of Italy, Vittorio Emanuele Orlando, was making a speech to a crowd of people just around the corner and the racers would have to wait until he had finished. One or two timid protests were made, but were quite unavailing. The speech went on and on in the village square, but finally the racers were allowed to move on. To add insult to injury, they then found they had to tack on behind the Presidental procession, led at a snail's pace by a big black De Dion Bouton limousine. Not until the President's cortege had turned off into a side road were they permitted to dash off and continue the race.

In 1920 Ferrari left CMN for Alfa Romeo, and Sivocci followed him there shortly afterwards, both taking part in competitions for their new employer.

In 1920 there came together the first generation of great Alfa Romeo drivers, at this stage driving pre-war cars. Sivocci and Ferrari we have already met, whilst Giuseppe Campari had been with Alfa as a tester and racing driver from the beginnings of the firm, when he himself was in his late 'teens. A native of the village of Fanfulla, only about twenty miles from Milan, Campari in 1920 was twenty eight years old and

Above : Ugo Sivocci driving a wire wheeled 20/30 ES Sport on his way to 4th place and a win in the 4½ litre touring class in the 1921 Targa Florio in Sicily
Below : Giuseppe Campari with his mechanic Fugazza in the 1921 Targa Florio, in which he finished 3rd in his highly successful 40/60 hp racer

had not yet acquired all the rotundity for which he was so celebrated in later years. He also wore a little Charlie Chaplin style of moustache, which was no longer in evidence during his years of fame. Like Ferrari he was a lover of opera, but Campari really did have a good voice, and his oft-repeated threat to give up motor-racing to take up opera singing was no idle boast.

Thirty two year old Antonio Ascari, like Tazio Nuvolari, who commenced motor cycle racing in 1920, came from Casteldario, near Mantua, the son of a corn merchant who moved to Milan, in which town Antonio started a motor business, and became the Alfa Romeo distributor for Lombardy. He had come into prominence in 1919 when he drove a 1914 GP Fiat, which he had pre-pared with his mechanic Carlo Sozzi, to put up fastest times both at Parma-Berceto and in the Consuma Cup hill climb, held near Florence.

Parma-Berceto, held in May, was the first big hill climb of the year in 1920, and here Antonio Ascari won the 4½ litre class with a racing bolster tank 20/30, whilst Ugo Sivocci won the production class with a touring 20/30.

The most powerful and impressive Alfa Romeo taking part was a racing twin carburettor 40/60 driven by Giuseppe Campari. In post-war form the car was considerably cleaned up in appearance, though in 1920 this was mainly to the extent of being given a more modern radiator and bonnet shape. At Parma-Berceto Campari won the over 6,000cc class, and shared second fastest time with Meregalli on a Nazzaro.

On 13th June Campari had Alfa Romeo's first outright win with this car in the first Circuit of Mugello race, taking in the difficult Futa Pass near Florence, and run over a distance of 242 miles. A Diatto was second and Eduardo Weber, later of carburettor fame, was third in his Weber car. Campari's winning average speed was 37.8mph over the hilly and twisty circuit, and whilst in the same area he made third fastest time in the Consuma Cup hill climb.

In October Enzo Ferrari put up a notable performance in the Targa Florio driving a bolster tank 20/30 by coming second behind Meregalli's six cylinder racing Nazzaro. It was very windy and very wet, and Meregalli averaged the slow speed of 31.74mph because of this, 4 or 5mph less than normal at that time. He took nearly 8½ hours to complete 268 miles, four laps of the Medium Madonie circuit. Ferrari was only eight minutes behind, then nearly three quarters of an hour separated Ferrari's 20/30 from the third car, a Darracq. Campari retired.

The distinction between a car in the racing class like Meregalli's Nazzaro or Campari's 40/60 and one in the touring class, like Ferrari's 20/30, needs some explanation. Every car that ran in the Targa Florio had the traditional bolster tank and two bucket seats and pro-bably at least a couple of spare wheels, so there was little external difference between a tourer and a racer. If its chassis was in series production, how-ever, a car could run in the touring class, but if not it was a racing car. The 40/60 was no longer a catalogued car, and in the early nineteen-twenties Campari's 40/60 was undoubtedly non-standard, so it was entered in the racing class.

It seems that any model would be sold in bolster tank form for racing, and Ferrari has told how he ordered a G1 racing car from Giorgio Rimini, the Alfa Romeo sales and racing manager, although the G1 was hardly designed in the first place as a high performance car – perhaps this was why Ferrari never actually obtained delivery.

In November 1920 Campari on a 20/30 averaged 79mph over a flying kilometre at Gallarate, near Milan, winning the 4½ litre class and making fourth fastest time behind cars in the unlimited class, a Packard, a Fiat and an Aquila.

The ES Sport version of the 20/30, which went into production in 1921, was suggested by Antonio Ascari. It did not necessarily have to carry sporting bodywork, some of the cars were sold in limousine form, but it was very successful in sporting events fitted with light bodywork, and celebrated its debut at Parma-Berceto in 1921 where two cars driven by Ascari and Sivocci headed the $4\frac{1}{2}$ litre class. Campari's 40/60 racer had had some development work done on it for the 1921 season, and looked very modern at the time with wire wheels and a much smaller windcheating cowled radiator. The exhaust system was also modified. It made second fastest time at Parma-Berceto, sandwiched between the big Fiats of Niccolini and Minoia.

Campari, accompanied by his mechanic Fugazza, drove the 40/60 in the Targa Florio, backed up by three ES Sports in the hands of Ascari, Ferrari and Sivocci. The battle in this race proved to be between a 7 litre single ohc short chassis Mercedes which had been driven from Stuttgart to Sicily by Max Sailer, who must have braved the Abruzzi wolves, and one of the 1914 single ohc GP Fiats, driven by Count Masetti, modified by having a welded steel cylinder block in place of the original cast iron one. Never far behind them, though, was Campari, and at the finish Masetti won, followed just over two minutes later by Sailer, with Campari less than three minutes behind the Mercedes. Only a minute and a half later came Sivocci in the first 20/30 ES Sport, with Ferrari under a minute behind in fifth place. This was a close finish, as it took Masetti nearly seven and a half hours to cover the $268\frac{1}{2}$ miles, at an average of 36.2mph. Behind came several Fiats, Ceiranos and Italas, then a Diatto, a Ford and a Chiribiri, the latter finishing after a ten and a half hour drive. Ascari retired.

Sailer won the touring class, and thus the Coppa Florio, Campari was second to Masetti in the racing class, and Sivocci and Ferrari were first and second in the $4\frac{1}{2}$ litre touring class.

More success followed at Mugello, where Campari again won with the 40/60 and Ferrari and Sivocci were second and third with their 20/30 ES Sports.

Following on the Italian GP in September, a 'Speed Week' was held at Brescia. In some kilometre speed trials, the amateur Count Franco Caiselli averaged 87mph with his ES Sport to come second in the $4\frac{1}{2}$ litre class to Count Masetti's 1914 GP Mercedes, with its more sophisticated engine of greater capacity. Third was another ES Sport driven by a lady – the young Baroness Maria Antonietta d'Avanzo. At this time the Baroness also owned the ex-Ralph de Palma 12-cylinder Packard racing car, which she drove in the speed trials at Fanoe, an island off Denmark, but the big car was not running properly on the sands of Fanoe. In 1919 this Packard had belonged to Antonio Ascari, and had helped to instil into Enzo Ferrari his fondness for 12 cylinder engines.

The Speed Week ended with a 25-lap race over the 11 mile Brescia circuit with the odd title of the Gran Premio Gentlemen, even odder because Baroness d'Avanzo was driving in it. The race was of particular interest as Campari was entered driving the old 1914 twin-cam Grand Prix Alfa, now fitted with modified cylinder heads and bigger valves. Masetti drove the 1914 GP Mercedes, and it must have been heartening for Merosi when the 1914 GP Alfa led the race from the eleventh to the twenty fourth lap in front of Masetti, only to retire with a leaking radiator on the very last lap within a mile or two of the finish. Thus the 1914 GP Mercedes passed into the lead and won the race from a Ceirano and Baroness d'Avanzo's ES Sport, which carried Ramponi as mechanic. The Mercedes averaged 71.9mph, and the ES Sport over 67mph.

This was the Grand Prix Alfa's last race. We are told it had class successes in other 1921 events, but Campari obviously had more confidence in his 40/60 racer, perhaps due to the old adage that there is no substitute for litres. Unfortunately the GP car was not preserved.

A close-up of Campari's 40/60hp racer in 1921

MEROSI'S ZENITH

The first genuine Alfa Romeo, as opposed to a developed pre-war Alfa, had not been a success, but the G1 was hardly a very advanced conception. The ES Sport was still holding its own remarkably well in competitions, but something new was needed if Nicola Romeo's ambitions for his new marque were to be realised.

As early as 1920 Merosi had started work on this new design, which subsequent production figures show was the most popular Alfa Romeo produced up until the early nineteen-fifties. Known as the RL (Romeo Series L) the new model was still in the Alfa Romeo 'big car' tradition, but in sports form the 3 litre engine was able to produce more power than the G1's of over double the capacity.

By the middle of 1921 two prototypes had been fully tested, and the first introduction of the new model took place in the old Alfa showroom at 18 Via Dante in Milan on 13th and 14th October 1921. Subsequently it was shown at the London Motor Show at the White City in November 1921.

The engine was a six cylinder with a four bearing crankshaft, and a capacity of 2,916cc, 75 x 110mm, in the touring cars and 2,996cc, 76 x 110mm, in the sports cars. It featured overhead valves and a detachable cylinder head in the best modern traditions, and also modern was the fact that the engine and gearbox were integral, instead of the gearbox being separate. The gear-lever and handbrake were central instead of being on the right as on all previous Alfas and Alfa Romeos.

There were two valves per cylinder and the valves were in a line on one side of the cylinder head. There were no combustion recesses in the cylinder head, which was absolutely flat. Compression taps were fitted, valve clearances were adjusted at the tappet, not the rocker end of the push-rods as on a side-valve engine, though the actual clearances were checked between

Sivocci and his mechanic Marinoni in a 20/30 ES Sport

the tops of the push-rods and the rockers. There was no pressure feed to the rocker gear, lubrication was effected here by frequent squirting of light oil on to felt pads in the rocker pedestals from a beautiful oil can with the Alfa Romeo badge stamped on the side.

The touring car, which had a single carburettor and a compression ratio of 5.2 to 1, produced 56bhp at 3,200rpm and was known in Italy as the RL Normale, or RLN, and in England as the 21/70hp. It had an 11ft 3ins wheelbase, weighed 36cwt and was capable of 68mph.

The sports car, with two carburettors and a 5.52 to 1 compression ratio, produced 71bhp at 3,500rpm and was known in Italy as the RL Sport, or RLS, and in England as the 22/90hp. The wheelbase was 10ft 3ins, weight was 35cwt and maximum speed was 75mph.

Knock-on wire wheels were fitted to the RLS and wire or artillery to the RLN, but front wheel brakes were not introduced until September 1923. On the early cars the foot pedal operated the transmission brake on the open propeller shaft behind the gearbox and the handbrake worked on the rear wheels. It was necessary to keep the front propellor shaft universal joint well lubricated, as the handbook warned that on long descents the brake drum would reach a very high temperature, which was partly transmitted to the Cardan joint.

Although it is hard to credit it today, the early cars had unlined cast-iron brake shoes, so that there was plenty of audible warning when a driver was trying to stop, even if he was not succeeding. The English importers used to exchange these unlined shoes for lined ones.

The RLN touring cars had flat, squarish, radiators, whilst the RLS models were given extremely handsome pointed radiators, which were rather in vogue on the Continent at this time, with an Alfa Romeo badge on each side of the point. On early cars these badges were attached to the top

Ugo Sivocci and his mechanic Guatta won the 1923 Targa Florio in this 6 cylinder RLTF Alfa Romeo

of the honeycomb, actually made up of square section holes, but on most of the cars produced they were on the radiator surround, and looked very effective indeed. The Grand Prix 4½ litre Alfa had also been fitted with two badges, one on each shoulder of its radiator cowl, whilst Campari's 40/60 racer had the single badge on the radiator surround in 1921, but fixed to the grille in 1922.

In 1922 the 20/30 ES Sports were still the mainstay of Alfa Romeo racing, and Count Caiselli and another amateur called Testi led the 4½ litre class at Parma-Berceto in May, whilst earlier in the year the professional Ascari made fastest time at the Gargnano-Tignale hill climb held near Lake Garda.

When Campari had had his great win at Mugello with the 40/60 in 1920, a driver called Tarabusi had come second to him driving a Turin built Diatto. In the 1922 Targa Florio, held in April, Tarabusi was entrusted with an experimental version of the RL, a bolster tank two seater with a pointed radiator quite unlike those on the production cars. His riding mechanic was Guatta, but unfortunately they retired

on the first lap after colliding with a rock that had fallen into the roadway.

The other works Alfa Romeo entries consisted of three 20/30 ES Sports driven by Ascari, Sivocci (with Marinoni as mechanic) and Ferrari, and Campari with the 40/60 racer which, unlike the 20/30s, was equipped with front mudguards. Baroness d'Avanzo in her ES Sport 20/30 returned to the fray wearing a red costume, a red cap and a flowing red veil. She had driven a Buick in that wet and windy 1920 Targa Florio race but retired, and she had no better luck in the 1922 race. Her riding mechanic was Abele Clerici, who had many successes driving 1,100cc French Salmsons in Italian events. The Baroness is still a motoring enthusiast, and attended a rally of vintage Alfa Romeos in Italy in 1968.

Ascari was really the hero of the Alfa Romeo team, doing very well to achieve fourth place with his humble side-valve engine against much more sophisticated machinery, and beating the entire Mercedes works team, which had already spent a month practising on the course before the event with fourteen mechanics and six drivers. Lautenschlager and Salzer drove modified 1914 Mercedes GP racers with increased engine capacity of 4.9 litres and front wheel brakes and finished eleventh and thirteenth. Sailer

40

and Werner had supercharged short chassis six cylinder 28/95 models of 7 litres capacity and came sixth and eighth, whilst the two 1½ litre supercharged cars of Scheef and Minoia were less successful, Scheef finishing twentieth and Minoia retiring.

The winner of the race was Count Masetti, who beat the Mercedes team in his privately owned 1914 GP Mercedes at a record speed of 39.2mph, and he was followed home in second and third places by Goux and Foresti in the remarkable sports twin ohc 2LS 2 litre Ballots, similar to the car Goux had driven into third place in the 1921 French GP at Le Mans against all the 3 litre Grand Prix cars of the time. Only about fifty of these cars were produced.

Ascari's was the third touring car to finish behind the two Ballots, Campari, surprisingly, coming third in the racing car class behind Masetti and Lautenschlager, although finishing eleventh just behind Lautenschlager in the race. This shows how successful the so called touring cars were. Sivocci came ninth, Ferrari sixteenth, and Ascari and Sivocci were first and second in the 4½ litre touring class.

Ascari's performance is all the more meritorious in view of the fact that his car did not have front wheel brakes as did those of his Mercedes and Ballot rivals.

1922 was the last year in which Campari campaigned his old 40/60 racer. He made third fastest time at the Aosta-Great St Bernard hill climb behind Alfieri Maserati's Isotta-Fraschini and Count Conelli's Ballot, and then had extremely bad luck in two races. At Mugello, where he had hoped to do the hat-trick, he retired when leading on the last lap due to a valve breaking, and then precisely the same thing happened when he was leading on the last lap of the formula libre 250-mile Autumn Grand Prix at the newly opened Monza track on 22nd October.

Monza Autodrome had been completed in a very few months in a royal park situated some ten miles to the north east of Milan. The circuit was somewhat unusual in that it was composed of a road circuit and a high speed track (Pista di Velocita), the latter being the same shape as Indianapolis. At that time the curves at the end of the straights were only slightly elevated, later they were given proper bankings.

The ten kilometre circuit as used in the Grands Prix from 1922 to 1927, and also in the Autumn Grand Prix, took in both the road circuit and the high speed track combined, and the cars passed twice in front of the grandstands in the course of each lap, the road circuit passing under the high speed track at one point.

An RL prototype driven by Ugo Sivocci also took part in the 250 mile Autumn GP, a new racing version which became known in 1923 as the RL Targa Florio. Sivocci managed second place in the under 3,000cc category, finishing only ten seconds after Alfieri Maserati's Diatto, probably one of the 2,950cc four cylinder single ohc models. Campari made fastest lap in his 6.1 litre 40/60 at just over 85mph at a time when the lap record stood at 92mph – set up by Bordino's 2 litre Fiat in the Italian GP the month before. The race overall was won by André Dubonnet's bit 6½ litre Hispano-Suiza.

The veteran motor racing journalist Rodney Walkerley has said that the old historic Autodrome is today the most magnificent stage for motor racing in Europe, with its impressive woods of beech and acacia and avenues of stately trees. He has described how the sound of church bells comes over the breeze from the neighbouring villages, whilst on a clear day the hazy blue mountains stand like a permanent backdrop to the north.

The autumn of 1922 saw much activity in the design department of Alfa Romeo at Portello. New racing versions of the RL were prepared for the 1923 season, and also a pukka Grand Prix car to the current 2 litre formula known as the Romeo Grand Prix car or Gran Premio Romeo. This name was shortened to GPR and later to P1.

Merosi's assistant since before the war, Antonio Santoni, had actually been trained as a chemist, and perhaps it is surprising that a building surveyor and a chemist should turn out such successful cars as the RL racers were to prove.

Five of these cars were laid down for 1923, three with standard capacity engines and two with 78 x 110mm cylinders in place of the usual 76 x 110mm, giving a capacity of 3,154cc instead of 2,996cc. The racing cars were much smaller and lower than the production ones with little cowled radiators and a wheelbase of 9ft 3ins, a whole foot less than that of the RLS. The chassis were narrower at the rear with outrigged springs, and could have either bolster tank bodies with two spare wheels or else a streamlined tail. Weight was down to 19½cwt.

The engines had modified camshafts and lightened valve gear and dry sump lubrication with approximately three gallon capacity oil tanks, while the fuel tanks held twenty two gallons. With 6 to 1 compression ratios the standard size engines produced 88bhp at 3,500rpm and the oversize ones 95bhp at 3,800rpm. Maximum speeds were 90mph and 98mph respectively. During the season some of the cars were fitted with front wheel brakes. As they made their first appearance in the Targa Florio, these cars were always known as RL Targa Florio models, or RLTF for short.

They were the first racing Alfa Romeos to carry the green 'quadrifoglio' or four-leaf clover, painted on their red bodywork on a white background. This symbol has appeared ever since on all the works racing Alfa Romeos, and the quadrifoglio seems to have originated as a decoration on the plates attached to the pre-war Alfas giving engine and chassis numbers. It is an international symbol of good luck, and certainly worked in 1923 when Ascari, Campari, Ferrari and Sivocci, joined by Count Giulio Masetti, dominated many Italian events

led by their enthusiastic and able racing manager, Giorgio Rimini, the young engineer from Catania in Sicily, with his swarthy complexion and cigarette permanently hanging from his lips.

The first race for the new cars was the Targa Florio on 15th April, in which Sivocci and Ferrari drove the 3.1 litre cars, and Ascari, Campari and Masetti the 3 litres. The Targa Florio varied from year to year, sometimes having a huge field of international entries and in other years having a small field almost completely of Italian drivers. The 1923 event was one of the latter, only fifteen cars were entered in contrast to forty five in 1922, and the one serious foreign challenger was Frenchman Andre Boillot on a 4 litre sleeve-valve Peugeot, who had won the 1919 event.

The cars were sent off at the usual two or three minute intervals, but it was soon apparent that the new Alfa Romeos had the legs of the rest of the field, particularly after Boillot retired on the first lap when lying fifth. After a seven hour eighteen minute drive, Sivocci with his mechanic Guatta was declared the winner on his 3.1 litre car and Campari missed second place through running out of petrol on the last lap. Instead Ascari was second and Masetti fourth. Ferrari, like Campari, retired. The leading Alfa Romeos were split by Minoia's 4½ litre Austrian Steyr in third place, the rest of the field being composed of further Steyrs and Nazzaro, Fiat, Chenard Walcker, Bugatti and Diatto cars.

Sivocci averaged 36.7mph and his best lap was at 40.8mph compared with the 41.3 mph of Masetti's Mercedes in 1922, which had set a record average of 39.2mph. Sivocci actually took one and a half minutes longer to cover the course than he had in 1922 when he

Antonio Ascari in a 3 litre 6 cylinder model RLTF Alfa Romeo in the 1923 Targa Florio in which he finished second to Sivocci on a similar car with a 3.1 litre engine

finished ninth in his 20/30 ES Sport. His RLTF was fitted with front mud-guards, and judging by the amount of mud on the car shown in photographs taken after the race, he must have needed them, and this may be a pointer to his speed being down.

On 6th May the scene shifted to Cremona in northern Italy, between Piacenza, the birthplace of Merosi, and Mantua, the home of Tazio Nuvolari, at that time gaining his first motor cycle racing victories. Here the first Circuit of Mantua race was held on a long fast circuit with a ten kilometetre straight. That Sivocci's 36.7mph average in the Targa Florio was no obvious guide to the speed capabilities of the RLTF Alfa Romeos is shown by the fact that Antonio Ascari was first in the 117 mile race at Cremona in a 3 litre car at an average speed of 83.37mph. He won from Alfieri Maserati's Diatto, while another Diatto and a Ceirano tied for third place. Ascari's car was timed at 98mph along the ten kilometre straight.

Mugello was another contrast in average speeds, the mountainous course bringing Count Masetti's win-ning average speed on a 3.1 litre RLTF down to 43mph over 242 miles. He was followed over the line by a 4½ litre Steyr driven by Count Brilli-Peri and Ascari on an RLS, who was twenty minutes behind and won the 3 litre touring class.

The rules for Italian races were slightly peculiar in those days. Horns were banned, and mechanics used to carry a good supply of old sparking plugs and bolts to shy at the occupants of a car in front, deafened by exhaust noise and unaware that a car behind was wanting to pass. Mirrors were not fitted, and riding mechanics were not always as watchful as they should be. Count Brilli-Peri made use of a whistle tied round his neck on a piece of string to make his presence known.

At Mugello there was a minimum weight of 9 stone 6 pounds (132 lbs) for the driver and the same for the mechanic. Although Antonio Ascari was considerably over this weight, the rules still said that his mechanic must weigh over the minimum. In the 1921 race Ascari's mechanic in the 20/30 ES Sport had been the faithful Carlo Sozzi, a little man with flat feet and prominent ears, but even with the cigar which was permanently clamped between his teeth he was still some 9 lbs under weight. To overcome this, Ascari made him put some strips of lead in his shoes and pockets, and Sozzi's exertions before the start made beads of sweat appear on his brow, though the weather that day was far from hot.

The River Savio flows into the Adriatic south of Ravenna and north of Cervia, and the first Circuit of Savio race was held there in 1923. It was another triumph for an RLTF, a 3 litre driven by Enzo Ferrari winning at 57.81mph from Weber's Fiat and Melloni's Ansaldo after a 166 mile race.

Mention has already been made of how the RLTF Alfa Romeo was the first to carry the quadrifoglio. At the Circuito del Savio it became the car which won for Ferrari his rampant horse badge that later appeared on all cars manufactured by Ferrari, and on the Alfa Romeos run by his famous Scuderia. After his Savio win he met Count Enrico Baracca the father of the Italian fighter ace of the First World War, Francesco Baracca, who had carried the rampant horse emblem on his fighter aircraft until the day he was fatally shot down. Subsequently Ferrari was introduced to the ace's mother, Countess Paolina Baracca, and it was she who suggested Ferrari should carry the black horse emblem on his car to bring him luck. This he did, afterwards adding the gold field behind it, which is the colour of Modena. Ferrari still has the photograph of Francesco Baracca with his parents' dedication on it entrusting the horse emblem to him.

The month after his Targa Florio win, Sivocci won the 3 litre category of the Gran Premio Turismo at Monza over fifty laps of the ten kilometre circuit (310 miles) in a four seater RLS tourer

44

Two of the 1923 Targa Florio cars after the race. Note the mud on them!

at a 69mph average with a fastest lap at 73mph.

Masetti had two hill climb successes with a 3 litre RLTF. At the Coppa della Consuma at Florence held a week after his road race win at nearby Mugello, he made fastest time on a car which from a photograph appears to have front wheel brakes. At the Susa-Mont Cenis he won the 3 litre class, but was beaten overall by two twin ohc cars, Maserati's 2 litre Diatto and Deo's 1½ litre Chiribiri.

From September 1923 Alfa Romeo fitted front wheel brakes to their production cars for the first time, actuation being by long steel strips to a little sprocket and chain beneath each king-pin pulling down the operating lever via a short cable hidden inside the king-pin. Compensation was by a balance beam and differentials on cross-shafts beneath the front seats.

By the autumn three of the P1 Grand Prix cars had been completed, and were entered for the 1st European GP which was also the 3rd Italian GP to be held at Monza on 9th September 1923. They were clearly modelled on the most successful GP car of 1922 which was distinctly revolutionary in design, the six cylinder Type 804 Fiat, with its Type 404 high-revving engine, streamlined bodywork and small, very light construction.

The engine of the P1 had the same dimensions as the Fiat, 65 x 100mm, 1,991cc, these dimensions also being shared by the rear-engined Benz built under the same 2 litre formula. The P1 engine had several features in common with the Fiat including twin overhead camshafts, with the valves operated through fingers, and roller bearings. The cylinder block, too, was of welded sheet steel in two blocks of three cylinders. There were seven main bearings, whereas the Fiat contrived to have eight. Other differences were that the Fiat had one carburettor, one magneto and one plug per cylinder, where the P1 had two of each, and the P1 had its connecting rods lightened by drilling, there being six holes in each rod. The P1 had dry sump lubrication where the Fiat had wet sump and the P1 valve angle was 90 degrees

45

ALFAROMEO

14708

Count Giulio Masetti's RLTF makes a pit-stop on its way to winning the 1923 circuit of Mugello race, near Florence

A late RL Super Sport chassis

to the Fiat's 96 degrees. The Fiat had a 7 to 1 compression ratio and in 1922 developed 92bhp at 4,500rpm, where the P1 had a compression ratio of 7.3 to 1 and 80bhp at 4,800rpm was quoted though a contemporary power curve was considerably more optimistic giving 84bhp at 4,000rpm and 93bhp at 4,800. 105mph was given as the maximum speed of the Fiat and as much as 112mph for the P1. To spoil these comparisons a little, at the end of the 1922 season the Fiat engine output had been raised to 112bhp at 5,000rpm, and in this form it won the 1922 Italian GP at Monza. Even worse for the P1's chances, by the time of the 1923 GP at Monza, the six cylinder Fiat was outdated, and instead the Type 805 with Type 405 Roots supercharged straight eight engine had replaced it, developing 146bhp at 5,500rpm with a top speed of 115mph.

The P1 had similar streamlined bodywork to the six cylinder Fiat, with full undershielding, but it was a larger car with an 8ft 8ins wheelbase to the 8ft 2ins of the Fiat, and it also seems to have been some 3cwt heavier. It had four-wheel brakes, the pedal operating

all four wheels and the handbrake a transmission brake. On the Fiat the handbrake operated on the rear wheel drums and the pedal on all four wheels.

The P1 was a good looking car, capable of development, and though in theory it may not have equalled the Fiats, which were supreme in racing at that time, given the reliability which Merosi's designs always seemed to display and the skill of the Alfa Romeo drivers, it might have had a not unsuccessful career. It remains a mystery car, however, because in practice for the GP at Monza in September 1923, Sivocci ran off the road at the fast Curva Vialone, and was killed. All three

GP, driving with a bandaged hand.

Car production shot up at Alfa Romeo in 1923 in comparison with previous years, and one would like to think Sivocci's Targa Florio win contributed to this. Total production was 829 chassis, composed of 610 RL Normales, 215 R.L. Sports and 4 RM Normales.

The RM Normale was introduced at the Paris Show in 1923, and was really a three bearing crankshaft four cylinder version of the RL, using many of the same engine and chassis parts. The 75 x 110mm, 1,944cc, engine produced

6th Series 1925 RLSS 22/90hp with English bodywork by Vanden Plas

Pls were withdrawn from the GP as a result, and no P1 ever appeared in a race.

Fiat also suffered a fatal accident in practice, but their cars were not withdrawn. Bordino's car was involved and his mechanic, the tester Giaccone was killed. Giaccone had driven a special 1½ litre twin ohc Fiat 502SS with conspicuous success in the 1922 Targa Florio, challenging for the lead until delayed by tyre troubles and finishing fifth, and had driven in the Fiat GP team. Bordino was only slightly injured in the accident, and actually won the

An RLT Torpedo of 1927

40bhp at 3,000rpm with a 5.3 to 1 compression ratio, a little higher than the 5.3 to 1 of the RLN. Maximum speed was about 60mph. As will be seen sports versions were later produced, but despite a lower price these four cylinder cars did not sell as well as the more expensive six cylinder RL types.

1923 had been a successful year, marred only by Sivocci's death, but things were being planned for 1924 which were destined to bring the name of Alfa Romeo to the forefront of the world's motor manufacturers, a position which it has never relinquished to this day.

49

VITTORIO JANO AND THE P2 GRAND PRIX CAR

When a manufacturer is producing all-conquering Grand Prix designs, his rivals are tempted to copy these and/or attract some of the design staff away from the successful firm. One of the Fiat design staff was Luigi Bazzi, a small thin-faced man with a moustache, and a friend of Enzo Ferrari. At the 1923 French Grand Prix at Tours, the eight cylinder Fiats had had trouble due to stones entering the intakes of their Wittig vane-type superchargers, and they had been beaten by the six cylinder Sunbeams modelled on the 1922 six cylinder Fiats by the fact that Sunbeams had attracted Vincenzo Bertarione late of Fiat, to come to England and design their cars for them.

After this Grand Prix Bazzi had had a row with Ing Fornaca, the Fiat chief engineer, and at Ferrari's suggestion had joined Alfa Romeo. He was immediately assigned to Merosi in the P1 project and carried out much of the development and testing programme on this car.

Nicola Romeo was particularly anxious to produce an all-conquering Alfa Romeo Grand Prix car to wrest the crown from Fiat, and in this desire he was joined by Giorgio Rimini, Ascari, Ferrari and Campari. Their difficulty was in beating Fiat at their own game with the Turin firm's years of experience of designing and building successful Grand Prix cars.

In the opinion of Bazzi there was one member of the Fiat design staff who was not only a genius in the field of design, but was also an excellent organiser, quite capable of overseeing production and testing even to the extent of running the pits at races and working out the team strategy.

This then-unknown member of the Fiat racing department was called Vittorio Jano. He had been born in 1891 at San Giorgio Canavese, near

Count Giulio Masetti manoeuvres his 3.6 litre RLTF Alfa Romeo at the 1924 Targa Florio race, in which he finished second. The car in the background is a Ceirano

Turin, where his family had settled over a century before after coming from Hungary, where their name was originally Janos. They were a military family but with distinct technical abilities, as shown by the fact that Vittorio's father was in charge of one of the arsenals in Turin.

Vittorio showed every sign of inheriting all the family's traditional talents, and trained at Turin's Instituto Profesionale Operaio before being accepted in 1909, at the age of eighteen, as a draughtsman at Giovanni Ceirano's Rapid car works in the Via Nizza in Turin. He stayed there for two years and then transferred to Fiat, where his gifts were soon recognised by Ing Fornaca, and he worked directly under Carlo Cavalli, in the design department.

By 1917 Jano was chief draughtsman at Fiat, and became concerned with both racing and production car design. He had accompanied the Fiat team to the 1914 French GP at Lyons, and in 1923 he was in charge of the racing team.

The invitation to join Alfa Romeo towards the end of 1923 must have come as somewhat of a surprise to him. Ferrari made a personal call at Jano's unpretentious house in the Via San Massimo in Turin to discuss the proposition, but Jano was out at the time and his wife Rosina said she thought Jano was too much of a Piedmontese ever to leave Turin. When Jano returned home he said Nicola Romeo himself would have to approach him personally, a suggestion Romeo got over by sending Giorgio Rimini to Turin the following day, when Jano was officially signed up.

It was not the increase in salary that attracted Jano to Milan, but the fact that he was being given a chance to design and build a Grand Prix car to his very own concept. and control the team himself. Within a few days, Jano his wife and two year old son, Francesco, had moved into a flat on the first floor of No. 71 Corso Sempione in Milan.

Luigi Fusi, the distinguished Alfa

51

Louis Wagner in a 1924 RLTF

Romeo historian and engineer, who had joined Alfa Romeo in 1920, was one of Jano's design and drawing staff of ten responsible for the new Grand Prix car – to be known as the P2 – although two of those on the P2 project came over from Fiat soon after Jano, Molino and Bazzi.

Jano decided that the new car would be a supercharged straight eight, following the latest design trend set by Fiat. Work on it was started very soon after the P1's non-event at Monza, but this does not mean the P1 was a completely useless blind alley. On the contrary, development work went into one of the cars, which was used as an experimental test bed for the P2. Supercharging was applied to the P1, the output being increased to 118bhp at 5,000rpm and a top speed of over 125mph was claimed.

As early as 10th October 1923, much of the P2 engine design and drawings were completed, and although a complete drawing of the chassis never existed, once the different parts had been made they went together perfectly. This was a pointer to Jano's efficiency, in fact Ferrari has written that Jano set up an almost military regime at Alfa Romeo in order to get the P2 project through, thus obviously making use of all his hereditary gifts.

By the end of March 1924, the first P2 engine was running on the bench, and the first complete car was finished by the end of May.

In appeareance the P2 was not unlike the Type 805 straight eight Fiat, with 'bull-nose' radiator cowl and streamlined tail, though rather heavier looking. The engine had a two-piece cylinder block of welded steel sheet the cylinder head integral with the blocks. The twin overhead camshafts were gear driven at the back of the engine and revolved in ten roller bearings. There were two valves per cylinder operated through fingers, and the valves were set at 104 degrees. The bore and stroke were 61 x 85mm, giving 1,987cc, and the compression ratio was 6 to 1. The two-piece counterbalanced crankshaft ran in ten roller bearings with bronze cages, and roller bearing big-ends were also employed. Lubrication was dry sump, with a ten gallon oil tank under the scuttle.

The rear fuel tank held thirty two gallons, and the Roots type two lobe supercharger of Alfa Romeo design was situated at the front of the engine and blew air into the single Memini carburettor through a large ribbed aluminium pipe. The now universal system whereby the supercharger draws the mixture from the carburettor to blow it into the engine was pioneered by Sunbeam in their Grand Prix cars in 1924. The Alfa Romeo system was similar to that used by Mercedes, and not relinquished by them until well into the 'thirties. The Alfa Romeo supercharger blew at about ten and a half pounds pressure, and ignition was by magneto with one plug per cylinder.

Power output with the single carburettor in 1924 was 134bhp at 5,200rpm compared with 146hp at 5,500rpm for the Type 805 Fiat. With the two Memini carburettors fitted for the Italian GP at the end of 1924, output increased to 145bhp at 5,500rpm and the cars were very fast, 140mph eventually being attained.

The chassis was conventional, although in the interests of streamlining the front mountings of the rear semi-elliptic springs were inboard of the chassis members and they narrowed towards each other at the rear to remain inside the tapering tail. The four speed central change gearbox was attached to the engine and the propeller shaft was enclosed within a torque tube. The four wheel brakes were mechanically operated, on a similar system to that later used on the 1,500 and 1,750 sports cars.

Despite the fame of the P2, it is interesting to note that its full technical details were not revealed to the general public until the publication of Luigi Fusi's book in five languages 'Le Vetture Alfa Romeo dal 1910' in 1965.

Although following the trends set by Fiat the P2 was very much Vittorio Jano's personal design; the fact is that of all the cars for which he was responsible in his long career, the P2 was always his favourite.

The first car, at that time without any paintwork on the body, was tested by Campari and Ascari first at Monza, and then over the Parma-Poggio de Berceto road. On the 9th June it made its racing debut in the 200 mile Circuit of Cremona race, with Ascari as driver and Luigi Bazzi, who naturally had been on the design and development team, as riding mechanic.

There was nothing else in the race to touch the new car and it won easily at an average speed of 98.31mph from a Chiribiri and a Bugatti, and along the ten kilometre straight was timed at 123mph.

Jano had insisted that the existence of the P2 should remain a secret until its race debut, and the secret was very well kept, even the motoring journalists being surprised by its appearance at Cremona. Although the car was obviously meticulously prepared mechanically, the bodywork showed signs of hasty preparation.

With the launching of the P2 it might be supposed that the old push-rod RLTF racing cars would be discarded, but this was far from being the case, for in the winter of 1923/24 they underwent extensive development under Merosi, the engine specification now differing radically from that on the production cars.

With the Targa Florio and other Italian races in mind, five cars were prepared for the 1924 season, the big difference from the 1923 cars being that they all had seven main bearing engines. Three of the cars continued to have 76 x 110mm, 2,996cc capacity engines, but with an increased compression ratio of 6.4 to 1. These now produced 90bhp at 3,600rpm, and were capable of nearly 95mph.

More exciting were the two cars with 80 x 120mm, 3,620cc engines, which produced no less than 125bhp at 3,800rpm, and were capable of a maximum speed of 112mph. Each of these cars weighed 20cwt and they were fitted with four wheel brakes compensated entirely by balance beams instead of the heavier differentials on the production cars. The foot pedal operated the transmission brake and the handbrake all four wheels. As on the 1923 cars, gear levers were on the right. The radiator cowls of the 1923 cars were done away with and pointed radiators with two badges as on the sports cars were fitted, except that on the racing cars these were much smaller. Squarish fuel tanks were fitted at the back holding thirty-three gallons compared to the twenty-two gallon bolster shaped tanks or streamlined tails of the 1923 cars. The spare wheels were strapped behind the petrol tanks at an angle of about 20 degrees from the vertical.

The 1924 Targa Florio was a big international contest like the 1922 race had been, with thirty-seven entries, the race being over the usual four laps, but following this the leader after five laps was the winner of the Coppa Florio.

For this year, Italy's most talented amateur racing driver, the Florentine Count Giulio Masetti, was again invited to drive in the RLTF Alfa Romeo team, and the famous veteran French professional driver, Louis Wagner, late of the Fiat team, signed to drive both RLTF and P2 Alfa Romeos in 1924.

In Sicily Ascari and Masetti were given 3.6 litre engined cars whilst Campari and Wagner had 3 litre machines. The race was run on 27th April, a boiling hot day, and after all the cars had completed the first lap it was seen that Masetti was in the lead, having averaged a record 41.8mph for the 67 miles, and within half a minute of him were André Dubonnet's lightened 8 litre Hispano-Suiza and Christian Werner's works Mercedes, one of three four cylinder supercharged 2 litre cars developed by Ferdinand Porsche from cars which ran at Indianapolis in 1923. On the second lap Werner had taken the lead and Ascari

on the other 3.6 litre Alfa Romeo had come up into second place. Andre Boillot on a sleeve-valve 4 litre Peugeot was third and Masetti had dropped to fourth place, in front of Campari's 3 litre Alfa Romeo. After the third lap the order was Werner, Ascari, Masetti, Boillot, Bordino (1½ litre four cylinder twin ohc supercharged Type 803 Fiat) and Campari.

On the fourth and last lap Ascari managed to get a one minute lead over Werner and was all set to win the Targa Florio when his engine seized some fifty yards from the finishing line and the car spun round and came to a halt. Ascari and his mechanic, Giulio Ramponi, were unable to push the car over the line as it was up a slope, and after Werner had gone through the car was eventually manhandled over the line with the help of numerous spectators and soldiers. It was timed as finishing second, but was subsequently disqualified for receiving help from the military and civil powers, so Masetti finished second and Campari fourth, with Bordino third.

Werner continued for another lap to win the Coppa Florio as well by nearly nine minutes from Masetti. Bordino's Fiat crashed after being taken over by Nazzaro, so Campari was third and Wagner eighth after some mechanical troubles. Of the other Mercedes team drivers, Lautenschlager was ninth and Alfred Neubauer, famous Mercedes team manager of later years, was thirteenth.

In 1923 and 1924 many of the Alfa Romeo team drivers and mechanics had a habit of wearing red sweaters or shirts with 'Alfa Romeo' in large white script emblazoned across their chests. Caps and goggles were the popular wear for both drivers and mechanics – caps usually being reversed, though a photo of Masetti in the 1924 Targa Florio shows him wearing a cap with the peak to the front, perhaps to keep the strong sun out of his eyes.

In the other Italian races during 1924 Enzo Ferrari was the most successful driver of a 3.6 litre RLTF At Ravenna

Personnel at Lyon, 1924. Left to right, Wagner, Sozzi, Campari, (the winner) Ascari, Marinoni and Ramponi

on 26th May he won the Circuit of Savio race for the second year running, a race in which Tazio Nuvolari won the 1½ litre class in a Chiribiri. It was in front of the Church of Sant' Apollinare in Classe, on the Ravenna road, where the pits had been set up, that Ferrari had his first meeting with Nuvolari. A week later on his 3.6 litre Alfa Romeo, Ferrari won the Circuit of Polesine at Padua, over 186 miles, at an average speed of 57.21mph, and again Nuvolari won the 1½ litre class on his Turin built Chiribiri.

The first Coppa Acerbo race was held at Pescara on 13th July 1924, also known as the Pescara Grand Prix. The cup was instituted by Giacomo Acerbo, a university professor and cabinet minister under the Fascist regime, and named for his brother Tito Acerbo, a hero of the First World War who had been decorated in the Engineers. Giacomo Acerbo took a tremendous interest in the Coppa Acerbo race each year, organising it with meticulous care, and insisting on a full field for the Grand Prix and also for its accompanying sports car race, the Targa Abruzzo, which in 1934 and 1935 was a twenty-four hours race. The most unusual thing about the Coppa Acerbo was that Giacomo Acerbo made use of his cabinet rank to ensure that the driver who won the race each year was created a 'Cavaliere' in addition to winning the Cup.

At Cremona, where Ascari and Bazzi had scored such a notable victory with the P2 on its first appearance, Campari had driven a 3.6 litre RLTF, but had retired. For the Coppa Acerbo he was entered in a P2, and was a strong favourite to win, but unfortunately he burst a tyre and as he had no spare was forced to continue on the rim and fell so far behind that his car was withdrawn. It has also been said he had gearbox trouble. Ferrari, who had Campari's cousin, Eugenio Siena, as riding mechanic put up a magnificent performance against the 2 litre super-charged Mercedes of Counts Bonmartini and Masetti (similar to Werner's Targa Florio winning car) and won the 159 mile race for Alfa Romeo in his 3.6 litre at 64.95mph, becoming a 'Cavaliere' in the process. Bruno Presenti on a 3 litre RLTF won the 3 litre class at 58mph.

The previous month a relative of Antonio Ascari, his brother Giuseppe, had come second to a German NAG in the twenty-four hour Night Grand Prix for touring cars at Monza, sharing an RLS with tester Attilio Marinoni. This appears to have been Giuseppe Ascari's sole contribution to motor racing history, but was far from being Marinoni's, whose future performances in the Belgian twenty-four hour races at Spa were to bring him recognition as a racing driver.

1924 French GP at Lyon. Louis Wagner's P2 leads Dario Resta's Sunbeam round the Sept Chemins hairpin

GRAND PRIX WINS AND A WORLD CHAMPIONSHIP

Up to this time all the works Alfa Romeo racing successes had been on Italian soil, although their production cars had been exhibited at the great Motor Shows in London and Paris. The previous attempts at entering Grand Prix racing, in 1914 and 1923, had proved abortive but now, at last, a team of no less than four P2 cars was entered for the French Grand Prix due to be held over a circuit nine miles to the south of Lyons on 3rd August 1924.

This Lyons-Givors circuit was a shortened version of the one used for that classic French GP in 1914, fourteen miles to the lap in 1924 instead of twenty three miles, using the northern half of the old circuit with the original pits, which were sunk into the border of the road thus showing the origin of the term. The start was between the pits and grandstand just after the Sept Chemins hairpin. It followed the Route Nationale 86, through the outskirts of Givors, and then followed the valley of the river Gier for about two miles.

Instead of continuing down to La Madeleine, as the 1914 circuit had done, in 1924 the cars turned right to climb a mountainous and rough secondary road to join the 1914 course again at Pont Rompu (Broken Bridge). They then turned right along the straight switchback road known as 'Les Montagnes Russes' to descend the esses of the Piege de la Mort and down to the Sept Chemins hairpin. All the time on this steep descent they were in sight of the spectators in the grandstand on the floor of the valley, who thus enjoyed a fine view. Much of the circuit was quite narrow, and lined with chestnut paling.

Meticulous pre-race preparation on the actual circuit had largely contributed to the Mercedes win in 1914. Jano approached the 1924 race with similar thoroughness, and a month before the race was due to take place the supercharged P1 was being used over the circuit to help Jano decide on suitable gear ratios for the P2s.

The Alfa Romeo drivers were to be Ascari, Campari, Wagner and Ferrari, but Ferrari fell ill before the race so his car was withdrawn and only three cars started. Of these, two had streamlined tails, but Ascari's was in the Targa Florio tradition, having a stumpy tail with a spare wheel attached to the back. Perhaps he was mindful of the reason for Campari's retirement in the recent Coppa Acerbo race.

Jano and Rimini were early in the pits on race day, and the racing cars were driven down to the circuit behind an RLN tourer absolutely crammed with personnel.

A race as great, if not greater, than the celebrated 1914 event then followed for besides Alfa Romeo, teams from Sunbeam, Fiat, Delage and Bugatti were present, plus a Schmid and a single American Miller driven by Count Lou Zborowski.

After the rolling start behind a motor cyclist on a beautiful sunny day,

Count Brilli-Peri in his P2 before the 1925 French GP at Montlhery

59

The P2s before the 1925 French GP. Antonio Ascari was to crash fatally in No 8

Segrave's Sunbeam immediately went into the lead, and after the first lap Ascari was close behind him followed by Guinness (Sunbeam), Campari, Bordino (Fiat 805), Divo (unsupercharged V12 Delage), Resta (Sunbeam), Pastore (Fiat), Benoist (Delage) and Thomas (Delage).

On the second lap Bordino lapped in 12min 5secs (71.41mph) and passed Campari.

By the end of the third lap Bordino was in the lead, and Segrave went to his pit for a plug change. A duel now developed between Bordino and Ascari and Guiness and Campari, with Wagner on his own in fifth place behind them. The Type 35 unsupercharged Bugattis were having tyre troubles, but the Delages were well up. Goux's cuff-valve Schmid was slow and had engine troubles, and Zborowski's Miller after a good drive, retired when its front

axle was seen to be coming off. Then Bordino started having trouble with the brakes on the Fiat, but he raised the lap record from the 72.94mph put up by Campari to 74.6mph on the twelfth lap. Finally Bordino gave in to his brake troubles and retired, and neither of the other Fiats of Pastore and Nazzaro were in the running, Nazzaro eventually retired due to lack of brakes and Pastore crashing. Before Bordino's retirement Ascari had lapped at 75.47 mph, and he he was now in the lead.

On lap sixteen Ascari took four minutes at the pits to refuel and change his wheels fitted with balloon tyres, thus letting Guinness into the lead, with Campari twenty seconds behind him. At half distance Campari led after Guinness had stopped to change a wheel, but by lap twenty Ascari had passed him, and soon after this Guinness stopped along the winding stretch in the Gier valley after passing through Givors with a main bearing gone.

On lap thirty two, with only three laps to go, Ascari slowed and drove to the pits, and he and his mechanic Ramponi endured a similar heartbreak to that they had suffered in the Targa Florio back in April in their RLTF car. They filled up with water but despite winding the handle and pushing the car they could not restart the engine. The reason was obvious when water started coming out of the exhaust pipe – the block had cracked. So dramatic was this moment that the most celebrated motoring artist of the day, Frank Gordon Crosby, made it the subject of a painting.

And so it was that Giuseppe Campari and his mechanic Attilio Marinoni passed into the lead to win the race at 70.97mph from Albert Divo (Delage), who was only just over a minute behind, followed by Benoist (Delage), Wagner (Alfa Romeo), Segrave (Sunbeam), Thomas (Delage), Chassagne (Bugatti) and Friderich (Bugatti). In between changing plugs, Segrave put up fastest lap at 76.25mph, and Campari's drive lasted for just over seven hours, making today's Grand Prix races rather like sprints.

This race virtually saw the end of serious participation in Grand Prix racing by Fiat who, after supporting racing practically from their inception, now decided that the costs outweighed the benefits. The crown had indeed passed from Turin to Milan – though hardly without Torinese aid.

The Alfa Romeo team drivers returned to Milan in triumph by train, and messages of congratulation were chalked on the side of their railway carriage.

In contrast to the French GP, the Italian GP at Monza on 17th October was a comparatively dull affair, with a team of only four supercharged Mercedes with eight cylinder engines

Antonio Ascari in his winning P2 at Spa, 1925 with his mechanic Ramponi

Commendatore Vittorio Jano, the famous Alfa Romeo designer – a photograph taken in his later years

to challenge the P2s. Of these, Masetti's Mercedes offered some sort of opposition at the beginning of the race, then after a fatal accident to Zborowski's Mercedes at the Lesmo curve soon after the race was half run, the entire Mercedes team was withdrawn. Thus P2s occupied the first four places at the finish, drivers being Ascari, Wagner, Campari and the veteran Nando Minoia, with two Schmids and a Chiribiri trailing behind. Ascari's record average speed over 500 miles was 98.75mph, which stood until 192?, and his fastest lap was another record at 104.24mph.

Total production at Alfa Romeo in 1924 went up to 829 chassis, of which 443 were RLN, 176 RLS, 71 RM Normale and 76 of the new RM Sport model with a pointed radiator. This had cylinder dimensions of 76 x 110mm, 1,996cc, the engine producing 44bhp. It had dry sump lubrication, and a top speed of 62mph.

Two Memini carburettors had been fitted to the P2s for the 1924 Italian GP, bringing the power up to 145bhp at 5,000rpm, but this increased the fuel consumption. As the Grand Prix races

of 1924 and 1925 were 500 or 600 miles in length, it was necessary for more fuel to be carried, so a five and a half gallon tank was fitted in the scuttle as a fuel reserve, and the oil tank was moved from the scuttle to a new position under the passenger's seat. During 1925 the power output was increased still more to 155bhp at 5,500rpm.

In this latter year Alfa Romeo concentrated their racing effort entirely on three Grand Prix races with P2s. Even the Targa Florio was ignored, and the RLTF cars were sold off to private owners, their swan-song being Ascari's fastest time of the day at Parma-Berceto in a 3.6 litre at the end of 1924. One of the seven bearing 3.6 litre cars went to England, where it appeared in various competitions, mainly sprints, over the years until being sold back to Italy in 1969, where Count Lurani now owns it. Another 3 litre car with a four bearing crankshaft was raced at Brooklands in 1925 by a driver called Lanfranchi. This car remains in England, where it is raced today in vintage events by its owner, Christopher Mann.

Of the other 1924 racers, a 3 litre was sold to Gino Ginaldi, who had a successful 1925 season, being sixth in the Targa Florio, third in the Rome GP behind Masetti's Bugatti and Materassi's Itala, and winning the Coppa Acerbo at Pescara from two Bugattis. Today Ginaldi is an hotelier in Italy.

In 1925 Sillitti was a non-finisher in the Targa Florio on a 3 litre, and similar cars were ninth in the Rome GP (Bertocchi), and third in the Tripoli GP behind two Bugattis (Siciliani). Another 3 litre went out to the Argentine, and was second in the 250 mile Gran Premio Cordoba driven by Ernesto Zanardi, finishing ten minutes behind Tomas Roatta's Hudson and four minutes in front of Eduardo Estanguet's 2 litre Bugatti. In Italy Bruno Presenti on a 3.6 litre was third in the Coppa della Perugina at Perugia behind Materassi's Itala and a Bugatti.

1927 saw Presenti, who was Alfa

Romeo distributor in Florence, finishing fourth in the 3.6 litre at Perugia, Materassi's Itala winning this race for the second year running. The Itala was a special 4.7 litre using one half of a V8 Hispano-Suiza 100 x 150mm engine with a single ohc, and was very successful from 1925–1930. Also in front of Presenti at Perugia in 1927 were two Bugattis. In the same year Presenti in the 3.6 litre came third in the Circuit of Savio race at Ravenna.

In 1928 Sillitti on his 3 litre was sixth in the Coppa Messina, but he retired in the Targa Florio, and out in the Argentine Vaccario retired his 3 litre in the Circuito de la Tablada, Cordoba.

The last appearance of an RLTF in an international race was that of the ex-Masetti 3.6 litre car (possibly the same one that Presenti had driven) which ran in the twenty-four hour races at Spa in 1931, 1932 and 1933. In 1931 it was third in the sports category driven by Rouleau and Rouleau, in 1932 it won the 4 litre class driven by Texi and Narischkine and in 1933 it was third in its class driven by Matozza and Meert, remarkable performances for such an old car, and a real tribute to its design. Marcel Rouleau of 31 rue Scailquin, Brussels held the Alfa Romeo distributorship for Belgium, Holland and the Grand Duchy of Luxembourg.

The first race for the P2s in 1925 was the European Grand Prix on a then new circuit at Spa in Belgium. As Wagner had left the team to go to Delage, the thirty-two year old amateur from Tuscany, Count Gastone Brilli-Peri, was engaged to drive in his place after having shown his abilities by gaining successes with Diatto, Steyr and Fiat cars. The three Alfa Romeo drivers at Spa were thus Ascari, Campari and Brilli-Peri, and it is interesting to find that all three cars had Manx tails with a spare wheel on the back like Ascari's car in the French GP at Lyons. Bigger brake drums were fitted to the P2s for 1925, and a higher engine output was obtained assisted by the use of a special blend of fuel. From this year

riding mechanics were no longer carried in GP races.

Spa in those days, with two extra hairpins, was not the very fast circuit it is today, and the fact that Brilli-Peri retired with a broken spring also seems to show that the road surface left something to be desired. The race itself was rather a fiasco as only teams from Alfa Romeo and Delage entered, and Delage had fitted superchargers, but no inlet manifold blow-off valves. The result was that a build up of pressure caused their inlet valves to remain open and hit the exhaust valves, so that all the Delages eventually retired. This left Ascari to win the race with Campari second, and these two were the only finishers.

Not surprisingly, the Belgian crowd became rather bored with the race which, as far as they were concerned, must have mainly consisted of watching an empty stretch of road for the best part of over six hours, the race distance being 503 miles. Rather unfairly they started making bird noises and jeering the Italians who seemed to be having such an easy victory. Jano took umbrage at this, and made Ascari and Campari have an impromptu five minute meal at the pit whilst their cars were cleaned and polished, thus infuriating the crowd even more. Ascari averaged 74.56mph and made fastest lap at 81.5mph.

In 1924 the French version of the Autodromo Nazionale di Monza was opened some fifteen miles south of Paris, known as the Autodrome de Linas-Montlhéry. Like Monza it consisted of a banked track, or Piste de Vitesse, and a road circuit joined on to it. The 1925 French Grand Prix on 26th July was held on the 7.7 mile road circuit which included the northern turn of the banked track, and large money prizes were offered for the first time in European racing – 150,000 francs for first place, 30,000 for second and 20,000 for third.

The P2s driven by Ascari, Campari and Brilli-Peri, now fitted with streamlined tails, had to face competition

Unusual sporting saloon coachwork on a 1925 2 litre RMU chassis

from the V12 Delages (duly fitted with supercharger blow-off valves), six cylinder Sunbeams and unsupercharged straight eight cylinder Bugattis. Brilli-Peri succeeded in rolling his P2 during practice.

Segrave's memory of the race itself (he drove in the Sunbeam team) is that it was unpleasant because 'it poured with rain the whole time', though from other accounts this would seem to be an exaggeration. Nevertheless the crowd was small, about 30,000, for the 8am start and Ascari proceeded to run away from the field, backed up by Campari. Brilli-Peri stopped to change plugs early on and with Divo of the Delage team, who suffered similar troubles, was soon out of the running, though Divo retired while Brilli-Peri kept going.

On the twentieth lap it started to rain and Ascari, in typical 'garibaldino' fashion, refused to slow up, but took a gradual 120mph left hand bend just past Les Quatres Bornes link road on the return leg at his usual 120mph. The result was there was no hope of his getting round, the car turned sideways and went straight on, crashing into the inevitable chestnut paling fence at about 110mph. It then rolled over and

threw Ascari out, coming to rest upside down nearly three hundred yards from where it left the road. Poor Ascari died in the ambulance taking him to hospital in Paris.

The race continued, the accident having happened at quarter distance. Within the next two hours, the news that Ascari had died was confirmed at Montlhéry, and the two remaining Alfa Romeos, which happened to be making pit stops at the time, were withdrawn from the race, their drivers running up their engines first to show they were sound. At that time, half distance. Campari held a two minute lead, and Brilli-Peri was some nine laps behind him. Campari had seemed in an unassailable position, though there were still some 300 miles to go. In the end Benoist/Divo and Wagner/Torchy in two Delages came first and second followed by Masetti's Sunbeam and five Bugattis. After the race, Benoist and Wagner drove down to the spot where Ascari crashed and laid their victors' garlands of flowers there. Later a memorial was erected there to Ascari's memory, which still stands.

The last driver to complete the course, Jules Foresti on a Bugatti, drove for 9 hours 49½ minutes, whilst it took the winning car 8 hours 54 minutes to cover the 621 miles. In the process Divo, who shared the wheel of the

1925 RM Sport 2 litre 4 cylinder with Torpedo bodywork

winning car after his own car retired, beat Ascari's lap record by one second.

Before the Italian GP at Monza on 6th September, a new driver was given a trial there on the first of the month in a P2. This was the champion motor cyclist Tazio Nuvolari, whose driving of a 1½ litre Chiribiri had so impressed Ferrari. In the trial, Nuvolari had been going progressively faster driving the P2, a strange looking figure at the wheel wearing his motor cycle crash helmet, when on his eigth lap the gearbox seized as he was coming out of a bend. Instinctively he de-clutched, but, like others before and after him, made the depressing discovery that de-clutching when a gearbox has seized makes not an atom of difference. The car spun round, hit a tree with its tail, and ended up right off the track. That night Nuvolari regained consciousness in a Monza hospital and was told he could expect a month in bed. Two weeks later he had the doctors bandage him up so that he could be placed on a motor cycle in the riding position, and was carried on to his 350cc Bianchi at the start of the 4th Grand Prix of the Nations at Monza on 13th Sepember. He won his class in a 190 mile race, and

put up a faster average than the 500cc machines, which were set to run an extra 100km, actually beating the 500cc lap record which had stood for two years.

Alfa Romeo had entered Campari and Brilli-Peri to drive in the 1925 Italian GP, but were lacking a third driver to replace the much mourned Ascari.

1925 was the first year a World Championship of Manufacturers was held in Grand Prix racing, and was decided on a complicated points system from the results of four races – the Indianapolis 500 and the Grands Prix of Europe at Spa, France and Italy. Thus the Italian GP was the decider, but Delage, though well in the running for the Championship, chose to ignore it and took part instead in the San Sebastion GP two weeks later where Bugatti fielded a team and Sunbeam entered one car. Delage had a walkover here. Sunbeam also ignored the Italian GP, but Bugatti entered three straight eight cylinder cars in a special 1½ litre voiturette class run concurrently, preparatory to the new 1½ litre GP formula for 1926. Surprisingly, perhaps, the American winners of the Indianapolis 500, Duesenberg, took up the challenge and two cars appeared at Monza to be driven by Tommy Milton and Peter Kreis, their single-seater cockpits bulging in an unseemly manner around the driver to make them comply with the European two seater width regulation, although the drivers still sat centrally in the chassis. The winner at Indianapolis, Peter de Paolo, nephew of Ralph de Palma, refused an invitation to bring his Duesenberg to Indianapolis, but accepted what must have been a surprise invitation from Alfa Romeo to drive the third P2.

The P2s now had shortened tails with three vertical slits in the point, a modification which first appeared at Montlhéry.

Although Campari led away from the start of the 497 mile Italian GP, it was Peter Kreis on his straight eight centrifugally blown Duesenberg who was in front on the second lap. On this lap he put up the fastest lap of the race, 103.212mph, then, like a meteorite which glows brilliantly and quickly dies out, he crashed at Lesmo on his next lap and his race was finished. Campari led until almost half distance, when he lost time on a pit stop, then Brilli-Peri, making up for his indifferent performances at Spa and Montlhéry, took over a lead he never lost to win from Campari by nineteen minutes. Costantini was a commendable third eleven minutes later in the little Bugatti, then came Milton's Duesenberg two minutes behind the Bugatti and De Paolo's P2 one and a half minutes later, slowed by the fact his car was only running on one carburettor. Brilli-Peri's winning average speed of 94.7mph was 4mph slower than Ascari's speed the previous year.

As a result of this race Alfa Romeo were confirmed as World Champions, and from that time onwards the badges on all Alfa Romeo cars were encircled with a laurel wreath as a reminder of the exploits of Antonio Ascari, Giuseppe Campari and Count Gastone Brilli-Peri in 1925.

After 1925, when the new 1½ litre formula came into force, Alfa Romeo retired from Grand Prix racing and the P2 cars were sold. One went to a Signor Nasturzio of Genoa, who evidently intended using it on the road, for it was fitted with headlights, a bulb horn, and a spare wheel on either side of the tail, though no mudguards. The cars were raced in independent hands in formula libre races and sprints up to and including 1930, when the works again ran a team, as will be seen.

If 1925 was an annus mirabilis for Jano in the racing world, it was the same for Merosi in the production field so far as the number of Alfa Romeo cars to come from the Portello works was concerned. In this year no less than 1,110 chassis were built, a production record which was not to be surpassed until 1951, when 1,277 cars were produced.

Two improved RL cars came out this year, the RL Super Sport and the RL Turismo, replacing the RLS and RLN. The RLT, or 22/70hp in England, had the 76mm bore of the sports cars instead of the 75mm of the RLN and produced 61bhp at 3,200rpm to the 56hbp of the RLN. The compression ratio was lowered slightly to 5 to 1 from 5.2 to 1, but the gearing of the car was raised and maximum speed increased by another three miles per hour to just over 70mph.

The RLSS, or 22/90hp in England, remains Merosi's most famous design, though today only about twelve cars exist throughout the world of the 392 originally built. On this model dry sump lubrication as on the Targa Florio cars replaced the wet sump of the RLS, and the power was increased from 71bhp at 3,500rpm to 83bhp at 3,600rpm, and maximum speed went up from 75mph to over 80mph.

These cars had delightful road holding and steering, an obvious legacy of Merosi's experience in designing successful cars for races like the Targa Florio and the Circuit of Mugello. The 7th Series cars from 1926 onwards were fitted with larger brake drums, and the braking was very good on them. The chassis cost £725 in England in 1925 when the Speed Model 3 litre Bentley chassis cost £925, but

the rate of exchange in those days favoured the English buyer. These English buyers found the 3rd gear of the RLSS on the low side, and higher ratio gears could be fitted, and also a right hand gearchange as an extra by Alfa Romeo British Sales Ltd handled by F W Stiles in Baker Street, London – not at No. 221B, but at No. 54 and later at 1-3 Baker Street.

The four cylinder 2 litre RMU also appeared this year, rather similar to the RMS, but with a wet sump and a longer wheelbase. The 'U' stood for 'Unificato', implying that the model was a combination of the RMN and RMS, which it replaced, having roughly the performance of the RMS thanks to an

The driver of this RM Sport, seen here on Fingle Bridge hill in a Brighton-Beer trial is Marcus Chambers, Chambers won over 30 awards in trials with this 1925 car in the 1930s

extra 4bhp with the roominess of the RMN.

In 1925 259 RLN chassis were produced, 143 RLS, 56 RMN, 53 RMS, 105 RMU, 195 RLT and 304 RLSS.

In the autumn of 1924, Jano was instructed to design a high performance medium capacity road-going Alfa Romeo, and the first chassis was exhibited in April 1925 at the Milan Show, and later at the Paris and London Motor Shows.

JANO'S SIX CYLINDER SPORTS CARS

Guiseppe Merosi's last new design for Alfa Romeo was a prototype track laying tractor with an RM engine intended for Army use. This was in 1924. In April 1926 he was replaced by Jano at Portello, and became designer for Mathis at Strasbourg. By the nineteen-thirties, when Jano was at the height of his fame, Merosi had returned to Italy and was in charge of the design of commercial vehicles for Isotta-Fraschini in Milan.

Most car designers live under a cloak of anonymity, and Merosi was no exception. When Alfa Romeo cars were famous in Italy, their designer was not, and Merosi's contribution towards the building up of the car side of Alfa Romeo was not generally known until some years after his death in 1957 at the age of eighty-five. How he viewed his break with Alfa Romeo after being so closely connected with the firm for sixteen years can only be conjectured. Ironically, Jano was destined to suffer a similar sort of dismissal in the future after fourteen years with the same firm.

Jano's first touring car design for Alfa Romeo was initially known as the NR (Nicola Romeo) model, and then as the 6C 1500. The engine was a $1\frac{1}{2}$ litre six cylinder with dimensions of 62 x 82mm, 1,487cc, and a single overhead camshaft. The cylinder head was non-detachable and the crankshaft ran in five plain main bearings in contrast to the four on Merosi's six cylinder cars. Valve stems were threaded and adjustment of the clearances was by mushroom tappets, a far easier system than the more common use of shims. Mushroom tappets were also used by Hispano-Suiza and Stutz and later on Wolseley and Morris cars with overhead camshaft engines in the 'fifties. On the 6C 1500 Alfa Romeo, a single carburettor, an Italian vertical Zenith, and coil ignition were used, the latter incorporating an automatic advance in

The German Willy Cleer with his RLSS after coming 3rd in the 1926 German GP at Avus with his mechanic Bonini

the distributor supplemented by a hand control on the steering wheel. The fan was driven off the end of the camshaft by a friction clutch which was also intended as a damper. A dry multi-plate clutch was fitted, and the four speed gearbox was in unit with the engine, while a torque tube was used in the transmission.

The smoothness of the engine was a revelation, and though not intended as a sports car – most of the early chassis being fitted with six seater coachwork on 10ft 2ins wheelbase chassis – a comparison with the 2 litre RMN of 1923 shows how advanced the 6C 1500 was. To begin with, although the wheelbase of the four seater shorter chassis 6C 1500 was precisely the same as the RMN's, 9ft 6ins, and the track a little wider, the total chassis weight was two-thirds of that of the earlier car, whilst the engine of half a litre less capacity produced 44bhp at 4,200rpm to the 40bhp at 3,000rpm of the RMN.

The 6C 1500 front suspension was unusual in that the semi-elliptic springs actually passed through the axle, as on many Bugattis and also the P2 racing cars. The rear axle was underslung, with the springs above it. The brakes were rod operated, the compensating mechanism being by balance beams enclosed under the gearbox. Actuation of the front brakes was by rods enclosed in the king-pins being pushed up to operate the brake cams.

The fuel tank was at the rear, with a reserve tank in the scuttle.

The heavier long chassis cars were credited with a maximum speed of 60-65mph and the shorter chassis four seaters with 65-70mph. The cars were expensive in England, costing £550 in chassis form in 1927, £750 for the tourer and £850 for the saloon. At this time a saloon Model T Ford in England cost £190 and a tourer £120. In chassis form the Ford's price was £100.

Jano being Jano and Alfa Romeo being Alfa Romeo, it was not long before a sporting version of the 6C 1500 was being produced, though no chassis of the model were made in 1926. In that

6th Series RLSS with 'Gran Premio' bodywork – Cleer's car in touring trim

year total Alfa Romeo production fell from over 1,000 in 1925 to 311, consisting of 173 RMU chassis, 126 RLT and twelve RLSS. In 1927 362 of the new 6C 1500 model were made, only six of these having the shorter 9ft 6ins chassis. Concurrent with these, the last of the Merosi designs were produced, sixty-six RLT and seventy-six RLSS chassis in their final 7th Series form.

It was in 1928 that the 6C 1500 Sport was offered to the public, its main difference from the touring 6C 1500 being the fitting of a detachable twin overhead camshaft cylinder head to the engine, with the valves inclined at ninety degrees. These valves were slightly larger than those on the single-cam engine, 28mm diameter instead of 26.5mm. Compression ratio went up to 6 to 1 from 5.75 to 1 and power from from 44bhp at 4,200rpm to 54bhp at 4,500rpm with a maximum speed of over 75mph. A single carburettor was still featured. The touring 6C 1500 was

now called the Normale, and most of the Sport chassis were fitted with four seater tourer and saloon bodies. The Sport chassis was actually a fraction longer in the wheelbase than the Normale, just over 9ft 6½ins instead of 9ft 6ins.

In 1929 the 6C 1500 Super Sport, with a similar chassis to the Sport was produced in small numbers, with two seater 'Spider' bodywork and with the option of a supercharger. In unsupercharged form with a 6.75 to 1 compression ratio, 60bhp at 4,800rpm was produced, but with the supercharger blowing at 5lbs 76bhp at 4,800rpm was available and gave a maximum speed of over 85mph. To accommodate the Roots supercharger at the front of the engine, the power unit was moved back 15ins in the chassis.

Very special were the 6C 1500 Super Sport cars with superchargers and fixed head engines. Only six of these were built especially for works racing, and they had sloping radiators. They had the same 5.25 to 1 compression ratio as the detachable head blown

Leader at Rome. Count Brilli-Peri in his RLSS in the 1927 Mille Miglia. He retired later with transmission trouble

cars and similar blower pressure, but still bigger valves, now 29mm in diameter. Power output was over 84bhp at 5,000rpm, and the maximum speed over 95mph.

In all, 806 of the single-cam 10ft 2ins six seater Normale chassis were produced and only 56 of the four seater 9ft 6ins wheelbase cars, which were really replaced by the twin cam 6C 1500 Sport, of which 171 chassis were sold. A mere ten Super Sport supercharged Spiders were built, and fifteen others without superchargers. 1929 was the last year of 6C 1500 production, when it was replaced by the famous 6C 1750.

The 6C 1750 models were produced during a period of five years, from 1929 to 1933, and 2,579 of all types were built, from Turismo to Gran Sport. Merosi's earlier RL six cylinder cars were in production for about the same period of time, and 2,631 of the touring and sporting types were built. The 1750 is the more famous Alfa Romeo, however, having had a whole book written about it (*The 6C 1750 Alfa Romeo* by Luigi Fusi and Roy Slater – Macdonald, 1968), and a current Alfa Romeo model has also been named the 1750 in memory of its ancestor. Unfortunately for the reader, with the coming of the 1750 the whole rigmarole of different models starts all over again, mainly paralleling the 1500 equivalents which they replaced, and quite closely resembled.

The one thing all 1750 models shared were cylinder dimensions of 65 x 88mm, 1,752cc, thus giving the model its name. The 6C 1750 Turismo paralleled the 6C 1500 Normale and also had a single overhead camshaft engine, with the difference that the cylinder head was detachable, and instead of the carburettor being on the offside and the exhaust on the nearside, both were on the offside on the 1750, thus facilitating hot-spotting arrangements. The long 10ft 2ins chassis was used, and as the engine only produced about 2bhp more than that of the 6C 1500 single-

7th Series 1926/7 RLSS with large brakedrums and Weymann fabric saloon bodywork

cam, there was not much difference in the performance, the 1750 being a trifle heavier. Mostly four and six seater tourer and saloon bodies were fitted on the Turismo chassis; two seater Spider bodies to special order only. By 1930 Alfa Romeo had set up a body shop of their own in the Via Traiano in Milan known as Carrozeria Alfa. These bodies were made of pressed steel so were quite light and fairly inexpensive, and many were fitted to Turismo chassis.

Those who have absorbed the foregoing dissertation on the 6C 1500, will quickly grasp the fact that the twin overhead camshaft 1750 engine in the 9ft 6½ins chassis constituted the model known as the 6C 1750 Sport, when first introduced. As most of these cars had four seater Carrozeria Alfa saloon bodies, however, Sport was not an entirely suitable name for them and by

1930 a much more appropriate name had been thought up – Gran Turismo. Turismo, then, meant long chassis single-cam and Gran Turismo shorter chassis twin-cam. The Gran Turismo was a 75mph motor car.

Like the twin-cam 1500, the twin-cam 1750 had inlet and exhaust on opposite sides of the head, and with a very slightly lower compression ratio, 5.75 instead of 6 to 1, it produced 55bhp at 4,400rpm to the 54bhp at 4,500rpm of the smaller engine, so again performance was very similar, though naturally more effortless.

It was in the realm of the Super Sport models that a bigger difference was made, in particular these cars had a shorter wheelbase in 1750 form. Again the name was revised in 1930 when what had been the supercharged Super Sport model became known as the Gran Sport, and all these Spider two seater cars had a 9ft wheelbase and sloping radiator. Power on the unblown model was increased from the 60bhp at 4,800rpm of the 6C 1500 to

Above: 6C 1500 single ohc integral head and block
Below: 6C 1500, known as the Normale with single-cam engine and as the
Sport with the twin-cam version

64bhp at 4,500rpm and on the super-charged cars from 76bhp at 4,800rpm to 85bhp at 4,500rpm, a bigger increase than on the other models, though only some 3mph in increased top speed was claimed, with a maximum of about 90mph.

The fixed head ('testa fissa') cars that were used by the works for racing were something very special indeed, the engines differing as much from the standard ones as had those on the RLTF cars of 1924 from the standard RL models. The main difference was that instead of having the five main bearings of the standard supercharged engine, these cars had eight, and could be taken up to over 5,000rpm – high revs indeed for a sports car in those days. In 1929 the output was 95bhp at 4,500 rpm, but in 1930 this went up to 102bhp at 5,000rpm, due to bigger valves, different cam profiles and a higher compression ratio, giving a maximum speed of over 105mph. The 1930 cars were also lighter in weight, about 16cwt.

These six cylinder Alfa Romeos can truly be said to be lineal descendants of the P2 Grand Prix car, having far more affinity with the small high revving Grand Prix cars of the early 'twenties than their chief rivals in sports car events – the Bentleys and Mercedes – which with their big single ohc low revving engines were reminiscent of the Grand Prix cars of 1914.

Of the successful Grand Prix marques of the early 'twenties, Alfa Romeo were the exception in translating their Grand Prix lessons into their road cars. Ballot had produced their twin-cam 2 litre 2LS sports car and Sunbeam their twin-cam 3 litre, but these were single models built in small quantities, and the ordinary road cars of Fiat, Sunbeam, Ballot and Delage did not particularly reflect their Grand Prix experience. None of them produced a supercharged road car except Sunbeam in the case of a few of the 3 litres, and then these pioneers of Roots-type supercharging in GP racing surprisingly fitted proprietary French Cozette vane-type blowers just like most of their rivals. Bugatti cannot be evaluated in the same way, as he was in business to sell his racing cars to the public, and, anyway, was a law unto himself.

The 1750 being in production longer than the 1500, various changes took place over the years. Crankshaft diameters were increased by 2mm from the 4th Series (the early 1750s were 3rd Series, 1st and 2nd Series being 1500s), and bigger lower geared super-chargers with a neater manifolding were introduced from the 51st car of the 3rd Series Super Sport in 1929. From 1931 a bigger clutch was fitted, 7ins in diameter instead of 6ins, to 5th Series Gran Sport cars. The supplementary petrol tank in the scuttle containing an Autovac was done away with on the 6th and final series Gran Sport cars in 1933, of which forty-four were built, when an electric petrol pump was fitted. These cars also had boxed chassis frames, synchromesh gearboxes with a freewheel, and tele-control shock absorbers. Prior to the 6th Series Gran Sport 1750 cars, some 265 supercharged Spiders were built and sixty unsupercharged. White-faced instruments were fitted to 3rd Series cars and black-faced thereafter.

A Solex carburettor replaced the Zenith on 4th and 5th Series Gran Turismo cars of 1930-32, but the blown cars all had Memini carburettors. The sporting Spider 1500 and 1750 models had an auxiliary oil tank in the scuttle from which the mechanic or passenger could supply extra oil to the engine, with the filler emerging from the left hand side of the car.

An unusual model was introduced in 1931 known as the Gran Turismo con Compressore, or supercharged Gran Turismo. It was virtually a big 8C 2300 chassis fitted with a detuned, though supercharged, Gran Sport motor, with Gran Turismo camshafts. Intended for commodious seven seater coachwork, it had big brake drums and a 10ft 4 ins wheelbase and was the only supercharged 1750 which did not have a sloping radiator.

The last model of the series was not actually a 1750 but a 1900 with a 68 x 88mm bore and stroke, the extra 3mm bore bringing the capacity to 1,917cc. Known as the 6th Series 6C 1900 Gran Turismo, 197 cars were produced in 1933 only. Using the 9ft 7ins chassis, the most notable thing about this car was that it had an aluminium cylinder head, and during the production run some cars were fitted with alloy blocks with steel liners. Like the only other 6th Series model, the Gran Sport, it had synchromesh on third and top gears and a freewheel. Normally produced in Carrozeria Alfa saloon form, the car did just over 80mph, and had a good reputation, though survivors are very rare today.

Many specialist coachbuilders built bodies for 1500 and 1750 chassis, of which probably the best known Italian ones are Zagato, Castagna, and Touring, all of Milan, and in England James Young of Bromley and Martin Walter of Folkestone. The Zagato Spider bodies were particularly famous, and were of all-metal construction, whilst James Young was probably the most prolific builder on Alfa Romeo chassis in England. As far back as 1914 Castagna had built an extremely futuristic looking streamlined body on a 40/60 Alfa chassis for an Italian Count.

For a time an Alfa Romeo branch in Paris assembled chassis to overcome certain import restrictions at that time, and instead of having 'Alfa Romeo Milano' on their radiator badges, these cars had 'Alfa Romeo Paris'.

The successes of the racing RLTF cars in the later 'twenties have already been reviewed. More striking successes were obtained by the P2 cars, some of which were bought from the works by the former team drivers who entered them in formula libre races running as independents. In 1926, for instance, Brilli-Peri came second in the 188-mile GP of Rome to Aymo Maggi's

Enzo Ferrari winning the 1927 Circuit of Modena in a 6C 1500 in 1927

Line-up of 6C 1500 cars before the 1928 Mille Miglia, with the winning team of Campari/Ramponi standing beside their supercharged Super Sport on the far right

Bugatti, averaging 61mph to Maggi's 62.08mph, with Count Bonmartini third in another P2. A Swiss driver, J Kessler, put up the fastest time in his P2 in several hill climbs and speed trials in his native country at such venues as Klausen, Fribourg and Zurich. In 1927 and 1928 Campari won the Coppa Acerbo at Pescara, his P2 being unusual in having a spare wheel attached to one side of the streamlined tail. He beat Maseratis, Bugattis and 1½ litre straight eight Talbots. Campari also made fastest time in his P2 at sprints and hill climbs in Italy and Switzerland between 1926 and 1928.

In 1927 Vittorio Rosa made fastest lap at 108.2mph in a P2 in the GP de Santa Fe over extremely rough roads at Esperanza in the Argentine, but his car retired from the race. Rosa was a somewhat mysterious character who was seen driving a four seater 20/30

ES Sport in the Garda Cup in 1922, an RLTF at the Solitude Circuit in Germany in 1925; and also the 3.6 litre RLTF car that came to England both at Brooklands and at Shelsley Walsh hill climb in 1926. He then drove an RLSS in a sixty-mile race on the 3km banked San Martin Autodrome at Buenos Aires in 1927, being narrowly beaten by a 3 litre Bentley driven by Englishman Eric Forrest Greene. In 1936 he came fifth in a Hispano-Suiza in the Sao Paulo GP in Brazil, and was last heard of living in retirement in the Argentine, after racing a 1½ litre Maserati there in 1947.

In 1928 Campari sold his P2 to Achille Varzi, but shared the driving of it with Varzi in the 373-mile Italian GP at Monza that year, in which they came second to Louis Chiron's Type 35 Bugatti, averaging 98.7mph to the Bugatti's 99.36mph. Tazio Nuvolari on another Bugatti was third.

Nuvolari and Varzi became great rivals, but began their car racing careers as partners. Varzi, aged twenty four in 1928, came from Galliate, near Milan, and was the son of a wealthy textile manufacturer. He went in for

motor-cycle racing, in which he could afford to buy the best machines, and became a star rider on Garellis and then on British Sunbeams. Nuvolari was much older than Varzi, being thirty six in 1928, and came from Casteldario, near Mantua, Ascari's hometown, where his family were landowners and farmers. Nuvolari also became a star motor cyclist, being 500cc Champion of Italy on Nortons in 1927. In that year he formed a Type 35 Bugatti stable with Varzi, selling some of his land at Ronchesana to obtain the finance. The contrast in the characters and driving styles of the two partners was remarkable. Nuvolari was volatile and excitable, wore peculiar clothes when he was racing, jumped around in his seat, patted his car, talked to it and pulled faces when he was driving. Varzi's driving style was extremely fast, but as impeccable and undramatic as his smoothly brushed hair, his face being serious and expressionless. Both were equally successful as drivers, though Nuvolari had an extra touch of genius peculiar to himself, enabling him to take risks and get away with them in a

way no other driver has before or since, and entitling him to a place of his very own in the motor racing firmament.

After Nuvolari had twice finished races in front of him, Varzi decided his style was being cramped, withdrew from the partnership and bought the P2, with which he was far more successful than he had been with the Bugatti stable. In 1929 he won the Circuit of Alessandria from two Maseratis and Baron Sartorio's 1750 Super Sport, the GP of Rome from Brilli-Peri's P2 and Divo's Bugatti, the Coppa Montenero at Leghorn from Nuvolari's and Campari's 1750 Super Sport Alfa Romeos, and the final of the Monza GP at 116.8mph from Nuvolari on an eight cylinder $1\frac{1}{2}$ litre Talbot and August Momberger on an SSK Mercedes.

The race over the Montenero Circuit was Nuvolari's first in an Alfa Romeo, and in typical fashion he drove in a plaster cast as a result of an accident in the Coppa del Mare motor cycle race over the same circuit a few days before. Brilli-Peri had driven his P2 in this race, but finished fifth behind Arcangeli's Talbot after clutch trouble. He had also

77

**The English driver, Cyril Paul, at the
St Martin hairpin during the 1928
Georges Boillot Cup at Boulogne.
Paul finished 4th, a similar 1500SS
in his team winning the race driven
by Boris Ivanowski**

been fifth in the GP of Rome, but he
just managed to win the Circuit of
Cremona from Varzi, averaging 114.4
mph over 200 miles to Varzi's 114.3mph.

Brilli-Peri's engine had been enlarged to 2,006cc, and he made fastest
time over the 10km straight at Cremona,
at 138.7mph, where Varzi on his 1,987cc
car achieved 138.1mph. Brilli-Peri's
time stood as the Class D 10km record
for nearly ten years. At Tunis in November, Brilli-Peri won the Tunis GP from

the Bugattis of Lehoux and Dreyfus, a
race in which Varzi retired.

At the end of the season, Varzi sold
his car, believed to have been Campari's winning car at Lyons in 1924,
back to the Alfa Romeo factory, where,
in company with two other of the old
teams cars (only six P2s had been
built altogether) it was completely
redesigned under Jano's direction.
With the bore size increased from
61mm to 61.5mm the capacity was
brought up to 2,006cc, and the power
increased by 20bhp to 175bhp at
5,500rpm. The springing was altered,
axles and brakes from 1750 Gran Sport
cars were fitted, a longitudinal slot was
made in the tail to carry a spare wheel,
the cockpit aperture widened, and the

whole look of the car altered by the fitting of a squarish sloping radiator, similar to that on the Gran Sport 1750.

Varzi raced his old car in its new form, carrying a riding mechanic, in the Circuit of Alessandria race in April 1930, and won it from Zanelli on a Bugatti and Enzo Ferrari driving a 'testa fissa' Gran Sport 1750.

A really big win was achieved by Varzi in the modified P2 in 1930 in the Targa Florio at a record average speed during which he put up a new lap record. During the race Varzi lost his spare wheel, and his mechanic had to beat out a fire at the back of the car with a seat cushion, caused by spilling fuel near the exhaust pipe as a result of trying to refuel from a can while the car was in motion. Jano had wanted to scratch the car, which had seemed too dangerous for the circuit, but Varzi had insisted on driving it.

The modified P2 team was not too successful otherwise in 1930, suffering from tyre troubles, whilst the road-holding was not quite up to their performance, so the Maseratis often had the upper hand. Nuvolari won a heat at the Monza GP meeting, and was third in the GP of Czechoslovakia after leading until six miles from the finish where he was passed by two Bugattis as steam escaping from his radiator forced him to slow. However, he did put up the fastest time at three Italian hill climbs, the Cuneo-Colle Maddalena being $41\frac{1}{2}$ miles in length.

Today Varzi's Targa Florio winning car can be seen in the Turin Motor Museum, whilst an unmodified 1924/5 car is in the Alfa Romeo Museum at their Arese factory, near Milan.

Turning to the sports cars, in 1926 there was only the RLSS to uphold the honour of Portello, and one surprisingly did this in the first German GP held in July under formula libre rules on the $12\frac{1}{4}$ mile Avus circuit, with its long parallel straights. Nearly fifty cars took part, varying from stripped sports models to Grand Prix racers, including Mercedes, NAG, Bignan, NSU, OM, Brennabor, Hansa, Talbot, Bugatti,

Austro-Daimler, Komnick, Steiger, Durkopp, Aga, BFA, Pluto, Alfi, Bob and GM. Most of the 244-mile race was run in the rain and, sad to say, there were accidents, some of them fatal. The race was won by Rudi Caracciola on a straight eight supercharged 2 litre GP Mercedes, then came Christian Riecken in a 2.6 litre NAG and in third place the only Alfa Romeo in the race, a stripped RLSS two seater with a long tail, driven by the German Alfa Romeo agent Willy Cleer with his Italian mechanic Bonini. A few cars were marketed with a similar body, called the 'Gran Premio'.

In 1927 the first Mille Miglia was held, that fantastic race over ordinary roads, in those days over a figure of eight circuit run in an anti-clockwrse direction from the start at Brescia, through Parma and Modena to Bologna. The route then struck south-westwards, over the Raticosa and Futa Passes to Florence and Siena and then to Rome. The return journey went eastwards, through Terni and Spoleto to Perugia, and then across to the coast, up through Rimini and Forli to Bologna again. The return to Brescia was via a semi-circle to the east through Ferrara, Rovigo, Padua and Treviso to return westwards to the finish at Brescia, by Vicenza and Verona.

Two RLSS four seater tourers were entered for the race by the works to be driven by Brilli-Peri and Marinoni, and Brilli-Peri's showed itself to be the fastest in the race and was leading at Rome. On the way across to the east coast on the return journey to Bologna, he retired with transmission trouble near Spoleto. Marinoni, at the front of the race, got much further before his car was struck with the same malady,on the last leg between Treviso and Brescia. The race was a triumph for 2 litre side-valve OMs, which occupied the first three places.

The 6C 1500 made its racing debut in June 1927, when Ferrari and Marinoni on unsupercharged twin-cam Super Sport cars came first and second in the Circuit of Modena race in front of a Bugatti, then Marinoni on a similar 1500

Super Sport won the Leghorn Cup and Bruno Presenti was second on another 1500 with Franco Cortese's Itala third.

The supercharged 1500SS made its racing debut in the 1928 Mille Miglia in which Campari, with Ramponi as mechanic, managed to turn the tables on OM, who this time achieved second place with a car driven by Mazzotti and Archimede Rosa while Strazza and Varallo's Lancia Lambda was third.

In the Targa Florio the supercharged 1500SS cars entered had typical bolster-tank-with-a-spare-wheel bodywork, and Campari did well to come second between Divo's and Conelli's 2.3 litre Bugattis. Marinoni retired.

In 1928 Alfa Romeo first started to make their influence felt on that peculiar institution, the British Handicap Race. A great deal of credit for the British successes must go to Fred W Stiles of Alfa Romeo British Sales Ltd, on whom all the burden of the organisation fell, the cars being prepared and raced in most cases under his sole jurisdiction He actually had to buy the chassis from Italy, thus involving himself in considerable financial outlay, and then fit bodies which accorded with British regulations. The Super Sport and Gran Sport chassis was designed essentially for two seater bodywork, which is why such cars never appeared at Le Mans as works entries, and the works would not provide Stiles with four seater bodies as also required in some British races for the over $1\frac{1}{2}$ litre sports cars. Thus the 1750 cars which ran in the 1930 TT had British four seater bodies. Where Italian drivers were used, Stiles had to travel backwards and forwards to and from Italy in order to engage them, and all the works would do was to provide mechanics to assist in final preparation a few days before the race.

1750 Alfa Romeos leaving the start of the 1930 Ulster TT, Campari in No 9, Varzi in No 8, Nuvolari, the winner, in No 10 and Callingham in No 11, with the OMs of Fronteras (No 15) and Ramponi (No 17) in the background

The first pointer to success in England was when Major C G Coe, who had driven Stiles's RLTF car in sprints, appeared at Shelsley Walsh hill climb in a smart two seater supercharged 1500SS and with a time of 54secs just managed to wrest the fastest sports car title from E R Hall's big old 4.2 litre 30/98 Vauxhall, a car which had more or less secured a niche for itself as fastest sports car at Shelsley every year.

The following week-end Stiles ran a team of Italian bodied Super Sport 1500 cars in the Essex Six Hours artificial road circuit race at Brooklands, one supercharged model driven by Giulio Ramponi and two unsupercharged cars driven by Carlo Bruno and Jack Dunfee. Ramponi won the race on handicap, averaging 69.51mph to the 72.27mph of the fastest $4\frac{1}{2}$ litre Bentley driven by H R S Birkin, and was actually fourth fastest on the road behind three Bentleys. The unblown cars averaged 64.85mph and 64.32mph.

In July a supercharged 1500SS won the twenty-four-hour Belgian Touring Car Grand Prix at Spa by the huge margin of 145 miles from two Chryslers. It broke the race record, though it had been led in the early stages by a 2.3 litre Bugatti, which subsequently retired. The Alfa Romeo drivers were Attilio Marinoni and Boris Ivanowski. Marinoni, who was now coming to the fore as a driver, was thirty six years old and came from Lodi, near Milan, the same district Campari was from. He had joined Alfa in 1910, where he came under Campari's wing, first as a mechanic, then as a tester, then as chief tester and experimental driver of prototype cars. He was of a very cheerful disposition and very popular.

Ivanowski had a romantic background, being an ex-officer of the Russian Imperial Guard who had narrowly escaped with his life in the Russian revolution. Later resident in Paris, he was an experienced long distance racing driver, having come second in the 1924 Bol d'Or twenty-four-hour-race in the Forest of St Germain in an 1,100cc EHP, and in 1926 he was

The Englishman, RS Outlaw, has trouble with his 6C 1500SS in the 1930 TT. He failed to finish

third in the Boulogne Light Car and Voiturette GP driving another small French car, a Ratier.

In August 1928, three 1500SS supercharged Alfa Romeos were entered for the 279 mile Georges Boillot Cup sports car handicap over a tricky twenty-three-mile-long circuit at Boulogne. The drivers were Ivanowski, Marinoni and the very experienced Englishman Cyril Paul, who had driven an Austro Daimler in the 1927 race at Boulogne.

The Georges Boillot Cup had come to be rather an Anglo-French institution, handicap and all, and Ivanowski's and Paul's cars were prepared at F W Stiles's Lorne Gardens Service Station in London, Marinoni and a mechanic called Perfetti doing the work on them, though Marinoni's own car must have gone direct to Boulogne from Italy. After two Bugattis and a supercharged four cylinder front-wheel-drive Alvis

had led initially and then retired, the team of Alfa Romeos moved into the lead and in the end Ivanowski won, a Salmson was second, then Marinoni and Paul were third and fourth. As the winning car came from England, this was evidently considered a British victory and 'God Save the King' was played after the race – though it is likely that the organisers did not have the Russian or Italian national anthems available in any case. Ivanowski averaged 69.65mph, and Birkin, who finished fifth on handicap in a $4\frac{1}{2}$ litre Bentley, put up the record average of 73.16mph.

The following month Ivanowski won that most extraordinarily bumpy race, the six hours Circuit des Routes Pavées held at Pont-à-Marcq, near Lille, in a blown 1500SS from an Omega Six and a Lancia Lambda, which must have been glad of its independent front suspension.

1929 saw the entry of the 1750 model into racing, and a blown SS version won the Mille Miglia in April in the hands of Campari and Ramponi. The Alfas did not have things entirely their own way, however, for one of the 2.2 litre side-valve OMs came second, driven by that talented crew Morandi and Archimede Rosa, in front of the 1750 of Varzi and Colombo; not designer Colombo, who was on Jano's staff, and destined to be chiefly responsible for the Type 158 Alfa Romeo and the 250F Maserati of future years.

The works 1750s entered in the 1929 Targa Florio were running on Elcosina racing fuel, as used in the P2s, instead of petrol in order to obtain more power, but Divo's 2.3 litre Bugatti won again, followed by Minoia's similar car, with Brilli-Peri's and Campari's Alfa Romeos third and fourth.

Stiles organised a team of five 1500 cars for the Brooklands Double Twelve Hours handicap race in England, collecting four of the cars new from Italy, Ramponi just won the race on handicap, with Ivanowski second equal to S C H Davis's Bentley. The winning car had a fixed head engine, and as this was not strictly within the rules, it can now be told that dummy nuts were welded to the cylinder head to fool the scrutineers.

Marinoni, this time partnered by Robert Benoist, drove a blown 1750SS to win the Belgian 24 hour Race at Spa for the second time running after the fastest cars in the race, a team of big Belgian Minervas, had skidded off the road in wet conditions. Second came a privately entered blown 1500SS, which had led for a time, driven by Captain George Eyston and Boris Ivanowski, with the 1750 of Rigal and Zehender third. Back in April, Zehender and Rigal had each driven a bolster tank 1750 in the first Monaco GP, Zehender retiring, but Frenchman Louis Rigal finished in ninth and last place behind

Tazio Nuvolari winning the 1930 TT in the rain on a 1750 Alfa Romeo

Above: 1930/31 Drophead Coupe body by James Young on 6C 1750 Gran
Turismo chassis
Below: 6C 1750 Gran Turismo chassis with bodywork by Carrozzeria Touring

Above: Supercharged Saloon. Weymann body on a 6C 1750 Gran Sport chassis
Below: Classic Zagato Spider bodywork on 1930 6C 1750 Gran Sport chassis

Varzi's victorious P2 passing through Campofelice during the 1930 Targa Florio

numerous Bugattis, a big Mercedes and a 1½ litre La Licorne. These vestigial Alfa Romeo racing bodies were designed by Luigi Fusi.

The following week-end Boris Ivanowski was in Dublin and drove a supercharged 1500SS in the 300 mile Saorstat Cup race, a handicap for under 1½ litre sports cars held on the Friday in Phoenix Park. His team mate Ramponi crashed, and E Fronteras with a privately entered 1500SS retired, but Ivanowski won the race from supercharged Lea-Francis opposition.

On the Saturday Ivanowski drove a privately owned four seater 1750SS which Stiles had just sold to a customer, but which was entered by him at the last moment in the big car race, the Eireann Cup, another handicap over the same distance. Ivanowski again won on handicap from a Speed Six and a blower 4½ litre Bentley. Over forty years later, Ivanowski's old 1750, registered UU 79, was successfully competing in vintage races in England driven by Richard and Patricia Pilkington, a young married couple who run a motor museum at Totnes, in Devon. The combined results of the two races constituted the 1929 Irish Grand Prix, in which Ivanowski thus had the distinction of coming both first and second driving different cars, the only occasion a driver has ever managed to do this in a motor race, even in Ireland.

No less than eight Alfa Romeos, all supercharged, were entered for the 1929 Tourist Trophy race over the Ards Circuit, near Belfast. Five were 1500s, the rest 1750s, and the official works team was made up of the 1500 cars of Campari, Marinoni and Eyston. Campari came second on handicap at 67.54mph to the 72.82mph of Caracciola's winning SS supercharged Mercedes of over 7 litres, only two

Achille Varzi in the modified P2

Mercedes and a blower 4½ litre Bentley putting up higher averages than Campari. The 1500 cars won the team prize, and the fastest 1750 driven by Lionel Headlam averaged 54.10mph and won its class.

The 1750 design really did prove its invincibility in the 1930 Mille Miglia, the big Mercedes of Caracciola and Werner could not keep up with the Italians, and the 2 litre Maserati of Arcangeli, which led after the start, retired. 1750 cars occupied the first four places, Nuvolari/Guidotti being the winners, followed by Varzi/Canavese, Campari/Marinoni and Ghersi/Cortese, with Pirola's 1500 winning its class.

Marinoni did the hat-trick in the Belgian 24 Hours race at Spa, winning at the record average of 68.50mph with Pietro Ghersi in a Gran Sport 1750, followed by the similar cars of Ivanowski/Cortese and Zehender/Canavesi. The Chiron/Bouriat 2.3 litre Bugatti had led until it retired during the night, and another 2.3 Bugatti driven by René Dreyfus and Schumann finished fourth.

At Le Mans Lord Howe and Leslie Callingham made a debut for Alfa Romeo with Howe's privately entered Carlton-bodied blue four seater, driven today in vintage races by Allan Cherrett. The car finished fifth behind two Speed Six Bentleys and two Talbot '90' cars. Ramponi, who was soon to take up residence in England, drove in the blower Bentley team.

At the Irish GP Phoenix Park meeting Ivanowski, Kaye Don and George Eyston formed the 1500 team in the Saorstat Cup, and Eyston finished second on handicap behind Victor Gillow's 1,100cc Riley. The following day, in a wet Eireann Cup, Campari was second between Caracciola's SSK Mercedes and Lord Howe's Mercedes, also on handicap. These 1750s had been entered for the race fitted with four seater bodies, of which Ivanowski's seemed to have a longer chassis, presumably the 9ft 6½ins. Campari's and Varzi's cars came direct from

Above: Inlet side of a 1930 5th Series 1750 Gran Sport engine showing the beautiful manifold castings and supercharger
Below: The engine of Varzi's 1930 modified P2. The name 'Romeo' as distinct from 'Alfa Romeo', was cast on both the camshaft covers on the P2 engines

Italy, and the word went round the English mechanics at Lorne Gardens that they were very hush-hush with seven bearing crankshafts, and only mechanics from Italy were allowed to touch them. We now know they must have had the fixed head engines with eight main bearings, the details of which were only revealed by Luigi Fusi in recent years.

Two more major victories went to 1750 sports cars in 1930 races – both handicaps. Louis Rigal and Freddy Zehender won the twelve-hour Spanish Touring Car Grand Prix from the 1750 of Colombe and Plate and Henri Stoffel's Chrysler, then there was an absolute grand slam in the more important (in British eyes, anyway) Ulster TT, where Nuvolari, Campari and Varzi came first, second and third in James Young-bodied four seaters on Gran Sport chassis. As they went so fast, one can only assume these cars had the special fixed-head engines.

In analysing the performances in racing of these six cylinder cars, it seems they were at their best in long races on fast courses, where they often beat bigger cars by making up in reliability what they lacked in flat-out speed, although undoubtedly they were not as fast round a circuit as a well driven Mercedes or Bentley of more than double the capacity. They did not shine so much in Sicilian races. In the Tour of Sicily race in 1929 the OMs of Rosa and Morandi came first and second, with 1750 Alfas third and fourth, and in both 1930 and 1931, Rosa and Morandi shared a 2.2 litre OM to win on each occasion in front of two 1750s. Fusi and Slater suggest that the torque at low revs of the OMs was a distinct advantage in an event where high speeds could not be attained; similarly in the Targa Florio, the extra power of the 2.3 Bugattis must have given them an advantage over the Alfas on acceleration up the hills and between the slow corners of the Madonie circuit. At Mugello too, in 1929, Morandi and his OM managed to come second to Brilli-Peri's 1½ litre

straight eight GP Talbot, beating a strong contingent of 1750 drivers, though Brilli-Peri reckoned he would lower his Talbot's time for the race in a 1750 the following year. Unfortunately there was no Mugello race in 1930, and Brilli-Peri was sadly killed at the wheel of his Talbot at Tripoli at the beginning of the 1930 season.

Strazza's Lambda Lancia on similar courses could challenge the 1750s, but Strazza seems to have been no mean driver.

The only British cars of similar capacity to approach the Alfa Romeos were the 1½ litre push-rod Meadows engined supercharged Lea-Francis and the 1½ litre supercharged twin-cam straight eight front-wheel-drive Alvises. The latter were really as advanced in engine design as Alfa Romeo or Bugatti and more advanced in chassis design, though due to the economic slump they never went into proper production for sale to the public. The Lea-Francis machines were very highly developed by 1930 while unfortunately lacking in reliability, and the heavier Alvises, though reliable, did not apparently quite have the speed of the Alfas. Nevertheless in the 1930 TT Cyril Paul's Alvis finished within thirty six seconds of Varzi after 410 miles racing, and, incidentally, was twenty five minutes ahead of the fastest 2.3 litre OM (Ramponi's) which was also supercharged.

An unblown 1500 Alfa Romeo was timed as being faster through the artificial corners than the Bentleys at Brooklands in 1928, but it must be admitted that the Alfa Romeo trump card was more often than not the extreme skill of their drivers. Although several of their English rivals in the TT had experience of road racing at Le Mans and Boulogne, none of them had the extensive Grand Prix, Targa Florio, Mille Miglia and so on experience of Nuvolari, Campari and Varzi, and the extra number of road racing miles which were behind this trio must have counted for a great deal.

THE YEARS OF VICTORY

Successful car though the 1750 was, there were larger cars which could beat it on speed alone, though it is probable its handling qualities were not surpassed at the time. To rectify this state of affairs, in 1931 Jano came out with a new model Alfa Romeo, known as the 8C 2300, just at the time when other manufacturers due to a world depression were abandoning such luxuries and wondering where their next meal was coming from. The 8C 2300 is the best indication that Alfa Romeo were not entirely dependent on the production of motor cars for their livelihood. The engine of this car had cylinders with the same bore and stroke as the 1750, 65 x 88mm, but as there were eight of them instead of six, the capacity worked out at 2,336cc.

The cylinders were cast in two blocks of four, made of light alloy with dry steel liners. To cut down torsional stresses, the twin overhead camshafts and auxiliaries were driven by a train of gears between the two cylinder blocks. The cylinder head was detach-able and in one piece, with phosphor-bronze valve seat inserts. The valve angle was 100 degrees.

The crankshaft was made up of two halves, with two helical gears bolted between them in the centre, one driving the camshafts through two intermediary gears and the other the Roots super-charger, oil and water pumps on the right hand side of the engine and the dynamo on the other side. The crank-shaft revolved in ten plain bearings, and the big-ends were plain as well. The throws were so arranged that the crankshaft was better balanced than the P2 crankshaft had been. Each of the two overhead camshafts was in two parts, bolted together with the driving gear, and running in six bearings. Valve adjustment was the same as on the 1500 and 1750 models, and ignition continued to be by battery and coil.

Dry sump lubrication was employed, with the oil tank under the passenger's seat on 1st and 2nd Series cars and under the driver's seat on 3rd Series. Twenty four 1st Series cars were produced in 1931, sixty eight 2nd Series and ninety six 3rd Series from 1932 to 1934.

The supercharger, which drew from a single Memini carburettor, gave 5–7 lbs boost, and with a 5.75 to 1 compression ratio output was 142bhp at 5,000rpm. Short chassis cars had an official maximum speed of 105mph and long chassis of 103mph.

The short chassis or Mille Miglia model had a 9ft wheelbase and the long chassis or Le Mans model a 10ft 4ins wheelbase. The semi-elliptic springs were outboard of the chassis, and the front ones did not pass through the axle beam as on the 1750. The front axle was located by two radius rods.

Rod operated brakes were on the same principle as on 1500 and 1750 models, but the brake drums were much bigger and completely filled the

Captain H R S Birkin's mechanic carries out some running repairs to the 8C 2300 at Comber during the 1931 Ulster TT

wheels. Both the back axle and gearbox were of the same design as that on the 1750 cars with torque tube transmission, the gearbox being integral with the engine, with a central gearchange. The large diameter multi-plate clutch was used, but the outer clutch rings were of aluminium alloy, lined on both sides.

The 8C 2300 had many characteristics of the supercharged 6C 1500 and 1750, the quick throttle response, light steering at speed and a general feeling of precision in every respect; the 6C engine may be compared with a sewing machine in its smoothness, and the 8C to a sewing machine with a deep exhaust note. The ride on the 8C was harsh by modern standards. It has been said that on cross-country journey the 8C was not much faster than a good 6C 1750. This could be true in certain cases, but it should be remembered that the 8C was available in various stages of tune, and it could become an 120mph motor car under extreme provocation.

A mention must be made of the superb finish of both 6C and 8C engines. With their fine ribbed supercharger casings and inlet manifolding and other beautiful castings in alloy, they came up to Bugatti standards for sheer artistic achievement, and in the opinion of some even surpassed them.

In 1929 an event of significance took place in Alfa Romeo history, the founding of the Scuderia Ferrari. Like many similar organisations of the time, this was originally intended as a pooling of resources by mainly amateur drivers, and a stepping stone for some of them towards professionalism. The Scuderia certainly did foster some new drivers, but as F W Stiles's experience showed, Alfa Romeo were always ready to pass the burden of racing their products on to others, even though designer Jano was not in agreement with this. From 1930 to 1932 the Scuderia Ferrari became more and more involved in Alfa Romeo racing in co-operation with the parent firm, but from 1933 it had considerably more autonomy in organising the racing of

Alfa Romeos, and was a fully professional organisation.

Some reorganisation of Alfa Romeo took place in the early 'thirties when the name was changed from Ing Nicola Romeo and Co to Soc Anon Alfa Romeo. Nicola Romeo had been President of the Company since 1925, but in 1928 he retired, and he died on 15th August 1938 in his villa of Magreglio, near Lake Como.

In 1933 the firm's capital, it being in considerable financial difficulties, was taken over by the government sponsored Istituto Ricostruzione Industriale. Thus, in a way like Renault in France in later years, it became nationalised, though remaining a private company with its own board of directors.

In the 'thirties car manufacture was but a small part of Romeo activities, when they were much concerned with aero engines, armament work and other diverse engineering activities including building commercial vehicles, some with diesel engines. They made Bristol aero engines under licence, and in 1930 Jano himself designed a nine cylinder radial aero engine. From 1929 S A Industrie Aeronautiche Romeo, Nicola's private company at Naples, built a light aircraft called the Ro (Romeo) 5, a two seater parasol monoplane with a fabric covered, welded steel fuselage and wooden wing, powered by an 85hp Fiat A-50 seven cylinder radial engine. It cruised at 95mph.

Fusi and Slater have told how Merosi's assistant, Antonio Santoni, built an aircraft in 1910 at Portello powered by a 24hp Alfa engine which was used for instruction at Taliedo Camp, Milan, and how in 1931 a supercharged 1750 engine was put into a Caproni biplane for the Round Italy Air Race, during which the aircraft was unfortunately damaged in a landing accident.

To get back to earth, the new 8C 2300 cars made their racing debut in the 1931 Mille Miglia, two cars being driven by Nuvolari and Luigi Arcangeli, an experienced racing motor cyclist and car driver and a native of Forli, of whom his mother once said 'He's a fine lad, but he's crazy and ought to be locked up.' These cars were short chassis Spider two seaters with civilised coachwork by Zagato, their oil tanks placed in front of the radiators between the dumb-irons.

The two new cars had nothing but tyre troubles and, after leading at Bologna on the return run, Arcangeli skidded on a wet road and terminated his race by hitting a wall. Campari then took the lead on a 1750, but was passed by Caracciola's SSKL 38/250 Mercedes on the run in to Brescia, and the German driver, benefitting from his experiences in the 1930 race, became the first foreigner in a foreign car to win the Mille Miglia. Nuvolari finished ninth.

For the Targa Florio two 2300 cars were produced for Nuvolari and Arcangeli, with bolster tanks, bucket seats and two spare wheels on the back. They were backed up by three 1750s, and Jano controlled the team with Ferrari. Jano had a radio link with the team's depots round the circuit, and fitted front mudguards to the cars in case of bad weather. This latter measure probably won the race, for it was run in rain and mist, the roads were a morass of greasy mud and Varzi, who led initially in a red 2.3 Bugatti had to slow down as he could not see properly due to his exposed front wheels. He was passed by Nuvolari who won on his 2.3 Alfa Romeo, and also by Baconin Borzacchini, a close friend of Nuvolari's, who was second on a 1750. Arcangeli, who had refused to fit mudguards, withdrew after receiving a stone in the eye and handed over to Goffredo (Freddy) Zehender, a native of Reggio Calabria, in the toe of Italy, who was destined to win the Circuit des Routes Pavées, near Lille, in a 1750 the following August.

An early Monza Alfa Romeo, with larger brake drums at the front than at the rear, during the 1931 French Grand Prix of 10 hours duration at Montlhery. Nuvolari is the driver

Above: The 2.9 litre racing version of the 8C 2300 engine in its advanced
form as fitted to the P3 GP car, showing the two small capacity
superchargers
Below: Inlet side of the 8C 2300 sports engine first produced in 1931

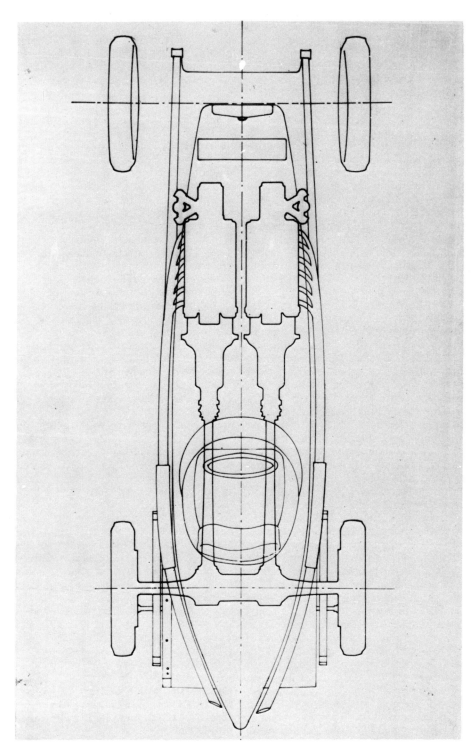

Layout of the Type A racing car of 1931

Le Mans saw the first Alfa Romeo win by a privately entered 8C 2300 driven by Lord Howe, the car's owner, and Sir Henry Birkin. The rival Bugattis and Mercedes had incessant tyre troubles, though a privately entered SSK Mercedes driven by Boris Ivanowski and Henri Stoffel was second, with a British '105' Talbot third.

In the Spa 24 Hours race there were no works Alfa Romeo entries, but a privately owned French entered 1750 driven by Pesato and Felix came second to the winning Mercedes. At Phoenix Park, Birkin's private long chassis 8C 2300 won the Eireann Cup from a Maserati driven by Campari and Ramponi, and Brian Lewis's Talbot '105'. This was the first time in twenty years Campari had driven a make other than Alfa.

Enzo Ferrari and Vittorio Jano accompanied three red long chassis 8C 2300 cars to Belfast for the 1931 TT, drivers being Campari, Nuvolari and Borzacchini, but they found the handicap system was not so kind to them as it had been to the 1750s in the previous year. Nuvolari retired on lap three with a broken piston, and Borzacchini was the hero of the race, putting up a record lap, and being beaten to the line by only five seconds on handicap by Norman Black's MG Midget. Campari finished sixth on handicap.

The Italian Grand Prix at Monza on 24th May, which was also the European GP, saw the debut of the Grand Prix racing version of the 8C 2300 sports car, which ever after was known as the 'Monza' Alfa Romeo. The Monza had a shorter chassis than the sports car, with a wheelbase of only 8ft 8ins, as well as higher lift cams, larger valves – necessitating dispensing with the bronze valve seat inserts – higher compression (6.2 to 1) and a blower pressure of 10 lbs, also magneto ignition. 178bhp at 5,400rpm was obtained with a top speed of about 130mph, and the main characteristics were a pointed tail, outside exhaust, and distinctive slotted radiator cowl. Early cars had smaller brake drums on the back than the front

wheels, and the passenger's seat partially faired over to give a $1\frac{1}{2}$ seater effect, but later cars had big drums all round and were full two seaters, being run as such in sports car races on occasions.

Another GP Alfa Romeo made its appearance at this Monza meeting. Known as the Type A, it was Jano's answer to the big engined racing cars produced by Maserati and Bugatti at the time. The Type A was a true monoposto, or single-seater, with the driver sitting centrally in the chassis. The power, 230bhp at 5,000rpm, came from not one but two engines – 1750s – side-by-side in the chassis, with two gearboxes, two transmission shafts and two crownwheels and pinions, one for each wheel. Instead of differentials there was a free-wheel unit at the back of each gearbox. The crankshafts revolved in opposite directions, cylinder heads were of alloy, crankcases were electron and the engines had eight main bearings. One gear lever worked both gearboxes, which had three speeds instead of the four of the production 1750s. Maximum speed was about 150mph.

Four of these cars were built, and they started off badly when poor Arcangeli was killed in one at Monza on the bend where, in 1923, Sivocci had lost his life on the P1. Arcangeli had been practising for the 1931 GP at Monza. Later the Type A cars fully redeemed themselves when in August, 1931, Campari and Nuvolari drove two cars to first and third places in the Coppa Acerbo at Pescara, Campari winning by two minutes from Chiron's Bugatti. Campari also drove these cars in sprints and hill climbs.

Much was learned from the Type A that went into the highly successful Type B, or P3, Grand Prix car which followed.

In 1931 Grand Prix cars could be of

Campari's Type A racing car, which had two 6 cylinder 1750 engines side-by-side to form its 12 cylinder power unit

any capacity, but the races had to last for no less than ten hours. In the race at Monza the new Alfa Romeos carried on the tradition set by the P2 of a win on their first appearance, the victors being Campari/Nuvolari, followed by Minoia/Borzacchini, with the first Bugatti, a Type 51 2.3 twin-cam, third. Campari broke Ascari's lap record with the P2, set up in 1924.

In the French GP at Montlhéry, a battle commenced between the Type 51 Bugattis and 2½ litre Maseratis, with the Monza Alfas holding off at a respectful distance. On a hot day, everyone was suffering from brake troubles and the Bugattis had an advantage when drums and shoes had to be changed because their drums were integral with the wheels. In the end the Chiron/Varzi Type 51 Bugatti won the race by twenty seven miles from the Campari/Borzacchini Monza Alfa, with a Maserati third; but the Alfas were the only full team to finish.

In the Belgian GP the Nuvolari/Borzacchini Monza Alfa was in the lead with two laps to go when it had to go into the pits with fuel starvation, and the Williams/Conelli Type 51 Bugatti won the race by six miles from Nuvolari when he had got going again. The Monza Alfa of Minoia/Minozzi was third and Birkin's sports 8C 2300 which he shared with Brian Lewis was fourth, a very stout effort.

Only six Monzas were built in 1931 and four in 1932. One of the 1931 batch was sold to Philippe Etancelin, a leading French amateur from Rouen, who did well against the Bugattis in the smaller French races.

It was clear, however, that the Monzas did not have the superiority over their rivals that had been enjoyed by the P2, so Jano got down to designing a Grand Prix car which it was hoped would be a world-beater.

Campari in an early 2.6 litre P3 Alfa Romeo with narrow cockpit in practice for the 1932 French GP at Rheims, in which he was a non-starter

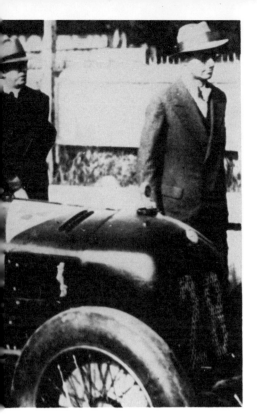

Nuvolari in the Type A

This was officially known as the Type B Monoposto, but for short it soon became popularly known as the P3, and it first appeared during the 1932 season. The engine was based on that of the 8C 2300, but the stroke was increased in length, giving cylinder dimensions of 65 x 100mm, 2,654cc. The cylinder block was alloy with steel liners, and the cylinder head differed from that on the sports cars by being non-detachable. The valve angle had been increased to 104 degrees and the valve diameter went up from 30mm to 34mm. Exhaust and inlet passages were on opposite sides to those on the sports engines, and instead of having one large capacity supercharger there were two smaller ones, one on each side of the driving pinion, each feeding its own bank of four cylinders with its own Weber carburettor. On the 2.6 litre cars the supercharger casings were exposed to the slipstream through

two holes in the bonnet side just above the chassis frame. Manufacturer's power output figures were 215bhp at 5,600rpm.

It was considered very important not to exceed permissible revs, and two rev counters were fitted to the dashboard as a double insurance against instrument failure.

The gearbox attached to the engine was identical to that on the sports cars, with the same ratios, and the multi-plate clutch only differed from the sports one by having the linings omitted to allow for three extra plates and alloy rings.

The gear lever gate was between the driver's legs, the lever cranked to the left of the gearbox, the clutch pedal was on the left of the gearbox, the brake pedal on the right and the throttle pedal was on the right of the brake instead of being in the centre as on the sports cars.

The most unusual feature of the car was the transmission, which consisted of a single differential behind the gearbox from which came two propellor shafts inside torque tubes, splayed out to form a V, and each leading to a bevel gear enclosed in an alloy housing situated under the chassis frame and just inboard of each rear wheel. This made for a very light back axle with low unsprung weight to assist road-holding.

The semi-elliptic springs at front and rear were outrigged from the chassis, braking was the same as on the sports cars, and big efforts were made to reduce weight by the use of aluminium and electron in the engine and duralumin for various chassis parts, so that the unladen weight was about $13\frac{1}{2}$cwt. Maximum speed was over 140mph. With their slim bodies, painted in the red of Italy of course, these were very handsome cars indeed. Six cars were built in 1932, with sufficient spares to make another three.

1932 was a wonderful year for Alfa Romeo, for not only did they win most of the major, and minor, Grands Prix, but the big sports car races as well,

Jano's eight cylinder engine designs really proving their worth, whilst it was also the year in which Tazio Nuvolari's genius at the wheel first received world recognition.

To begin the season, Borzacchini won the Mille Miglia in a 2.3 litre Mille Miglia sports car, the only Scuderia Ferrari car to finish, but, apart from a Lancia which was eighth, Alfas filled the first twelve places. These included a 1750 Gran Turismo con Compressore saloon, which was fourth driven by Nando Minoia and Renato Balestrero, finishing two hours behind the winner. This was the first race for Count Felice Trossi, President of the Scuderia Ferrari, whose 2.3 finished in second place with Marquis Antonio Brivio who, like Trossi, came from Biella, sharing the wheel.

The new P3s were not ready for the Monaco GP in April, which Nuvolari won on a Scuderia Ferrari Monza. The

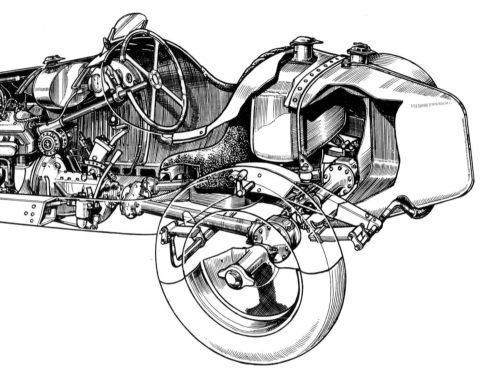

Scuderia had had the foresight to sign up Rudi Caracciola for the season, and he finished second with Luigi Fagioli's 2.8 litre Maserati third and Lord Howe's Type 51 Bugatti fourth. Nuvolari on a Monza also won the Targa Florio at an average speed not exceeded until 1935. Borzacchini's Monza was second and a Chiron/Varzi Type 51 Bugatti third. Caracciola was sent to his native Germany to win the Eifelrennen on the Nurburg Ring and set up the fastest lap, and to lose the Avusrennen on the fast Avus track by four seconds to von Brauchitsch's big aerodynamic SSKL Mercedes.

The P3s, two cars driven by Nuvolari and Campari, made their debut at the beginning of June in the Italian GP at Monza. Again a Grand Prix Alfa Romeo won on its first appearance, Nuvolari driving. His average speed for the five (rather than ten) hours now obligatory as Grand Prix duration was

P3 chassis layout, 1932

less than one mile per hour slower than Campari's lap record on the Monza model put up the previous year. Fagioli was second on a Maserati somewhat on the lines of the Type A Alfa Romeo, having two 2.5 litre straight eight engines side-by-side in the chassis, though with a single gearbox and propellor shaft. Borzacchini's Monza was third and Campari's P3 fourth.

Le Mans went to a special-bodied 2.3 Alfa Romeo driven for twenty-one hours by the French amateur Raymond Sommer, as his co-driver Chinetti became unwell. The Cortese/Guidotti 2.3 was second and one of the fine '105' Talbots driven by Brian Lewis and Tim Rose-Richards was third, with a 1750 in fourth place driven by Madame Odette Siko and 'Sabipa', whose real name was Louis Charavel.

A 6C 1900 saloon – 1933

The French GP was held for the first time on the Rheims circuit in 1932 and was a 1-2-3 victory for the 2.6 litre P3 Alfas against Bugatti opposition, Nuvolari winning again, with Borzacchini second and Caracciola third. The same trio defeated the 2.3 litre Type 51 Bugattis in the German GP at the Nurburg Ring, the order being Caracciola, Nuvolari and Borzacchini.

The indomitable Nuvolari and his P3 also won three Italian races, the Coppa Ciano at Montenero, the Coppa Acerbo at Pescara and the Circuit of Avellino, well backed up by his team mates against Bugattis and Maseratis. The only races he failed to win were the Czechoslovakian GP, where he had repeated ignition trouble and was third to Chiron's Bugatti and Fagioli's Maserati, and the Marseilles GP on that rather featureless track at Miramas in the Camargue district of France where Raymond Sommer had the effrontery to beat him on his 2.3 litre Monza Alfa

after Nuvolari had been delayed by a burst tyre.

Caracciola on a 2.6 litre Monoposto won the final of the Monza GP, and the Spa 24 Hours race was another 8C 2300 benefit, the first three cars being driven by Brivio/Siena, Taruffi/D'Ippolito and Earl Howe/Birkin. In France, privately owned Monzas driven by Etancelin, Jean Pierre Wimille and Freddy Zehender won the GPs of Picardy, Lorraine and Comminges against the Bugatti hordes.

Having proved their cars to be almost invincible in 1932, and as finances were in a poor state, the now nationalised Alfa Romeo company announced their withdrawal from racing in 1933, which must have sounded good news for Bugatti and Maserati. The Scuderia Ferrari still went on racing Alfa Romeos, however, but not the 2.6 litre Monoposto cars; Alfa Romeo put them into cold storage, refusing either to sell them or to lend them, even to Ferrari. Monzas were still plentiful, so Ferrari fielded a team of Monzas with their engines bored out to 2.6 litres, 69 x 88mm, and having Weber carburettors, with Nuvolari and Borzacchini as his chief drivers. Instead of the 'quadrifoglio' on the side, the cars bore the black horse on a gold background, the badge of the Scuderia Ferrari. Many private owners of different nationalities raced Monzas in 1933, so one begins to suspect the official figures – ten built in 1931 and 1932 – particularly when it is known that some drivers bought new cars in 1933. Caracciola and Chiron, for instance, formed a partnership with two Monzas, and the rising star Guy Moll obtained a new car in May 1933, while Phi-Phi Etancelin also bought himself a new car for the 1933 season. The answer must be that the Scuderia Ferrari converted some 8C 2300 sports cars to Monza specification.

That Bugattis still raced in hordes in France is shown by the line-up at the GP of Pau, where three French owned Monza Alfas faced thirteen Bugattis and one Maserati, and Etancelin finished third to the Bugattis of Lehoux and Moll after misfiring due to snow (repeat, snow) melting on one of his plug leads.

At the GP of Tunis seven Alfas raced against eleven Bugattis and four Maseratis, and Nuvolari and Borzacchini crossed the line first and second within a fifth of a second of each other, with Freddy Zehender on his new 2.9 litre Maserati third. Nuvolari had his second Mille Miglia win in 1933, this time in a sports 2.3, and the Lancia which annually got in amongst all the Alfa Romeos which annually filled the first twelve places this year came tenth.

Nuvolari had the most terrible duel at Monaco in his Monza with Varzi's Type 51 Bugatti. Nuvolari held the lead on 66 laps and Varzi on 34 during the 100 lap race. Then, on the last lap Nuvolari slowed with a burst oil pipe and his car caught fire, so Varzi was the winner with Borzacchini second and Dreyfus (Bugatti) third. Caracciola crashed and severely injured his hip in practice for this race.

At Tripoli Varzi won from Nuvolari by a car's length, but there were ugly rumours that this result was rigged by the drivers who received large sums of money from the winners of a lottery run in connection with the race.

This may not exactly have been cricket, but all was above board in England at Brooklands that same weekend where a member of the MCC, the Hon Brian Lewis, won the 260 mile International Trophy race on a 2.3 Monza with a Memini carburettor that had come straight from Italy. MG Magnettes were second and third in a race in which the handicap was arranged by having artificial corners of a different severity for the various capacity cars on a wide part of the track.

Bugatti cunningly sent his powerful 4.9 litre Type 54 cars to Avus, where the mere 2.6 litres of Nuvolari's and Borzacchini's Monzas could not match them on the long straights, and the Monzas dead-heated for third place five minutes behind the Bugattis of Varzi and Count Czaykowski. On the same day Etancelin's Monza won the Picardy GP at Peronne from Sommer's similar car and Lehoux's Type 51 Bugatti; then, the following week-end, Nuvolari won the Eifelrennen at Nurburg and 'Tonino Brivio won a rather second rate Targa Florio for Alfa Romeo.

It would seem that in France Bugattis were beginning to lose out numerically to Alfa Romeos, for at the GP of Nimes five Alfa Romeos faced three Bugattis, and the Alfas triumphed by taking the first four places; Nuvolari, Etancelin, Moll and Sommer.

In the French GP at Montlhéry, there were twelve Alfa Romeos, five Bugattis and two Maseratis. Nuvolari led on his Monza, broke his differential, took over Taruffi's similar car and broke the differential on that as well, which made him very cross indeed. Campari was driving a two seater Maserati with the latest 2.9 litre engine, and he just won from Etancelin's Monza which might have won had it not been slowed with gear-box trouble in the latter stages of the race. George Eyston was third in the Monza belonging to Bernard Rubin, which Birkin would have driven but for his fatal illness in 1933.

At Le Mans Nuvolari joined forces with Raymond Sommer in the latter's 8C 2300 Alfa Romeo, and they won by ten seconds from the Chiron/Chinetti 8C 2300 and a similar car driven by

The Hon Brian Lewis on his way to winning the 1933 Mannin Moar race in the Isle of Man in a Monza Alfa Romeo which was extremely successful in the leading British races of the time

Brian Lewis and Tim Rose-Richards. 8C 2300 Alfas were also first, second and third in the Spa 24 Hours race, Chiron and Chinetti sharing the winning car.

Misfortune continued to dog Nuvolari in GP races. At Penya Rhin in Spain, where the Chilean driver Juan Zanelli won on a Monza which is raced in English vintage events today by David Black, Nuvolari was delayed with carburettor trouble and misfiring, and in the GP de la Marne on the Rheims circuit he broke a differential again. This race was a Monza Alfa first, second

and third result against Bugattis and Maseratis with Etancelin winning from Wimille on their 2.3 litre cars and Sommer third on a 2.6 litre. Several private owners like Sommer had Monzas bored out to 2.6 litres like the Ferrari cars.

This third differential failure proved the last straw for Nuvolari, who left the Scuderia Ferrari and appeared at the start of the Belgian GP in a 2.9 litre monoposto Maserati, with which he promptly won the race from the Bugattis of Varzi and Dreyfus. He also won the Nice GP, and although Brivio won the Swedish Summer GP on a 2.6 Monza for the Scuderia Ferrari and independents Brian Lewis and Eugene Bjornstad respectively won the Mannin Moar race in the Isle of Man and the Lwow GP in Poland with 2.3 Monza cars, the Maserati threat was a worry at Portello, particularly when Nuvolari won the Coppa Ciano at Montenero from Brivio's Monza Ferrari Alfa by

Nuvolari and Sommer after winning the 1933 Le Mans race by 10 seconds

Above: A 1933 long chassis 8C 2300 with novel bodywork by Vanvooren
Below: Tim Rose-Richards driving an 8C 2300 Alfa Romeo in the 1933 Ulster
TT in which he finished third and put up the fastest lap

over eight minutes.

As a result of this, Alfa Romeo sprung a surprise by releasing the 2.6 litre Monoposto cars to the Scuderia Ferrari in August and Luigi Fagioli, 'The Old Abruzzi Robber', who replaced Nuvolari in the Scuderia, drove one to win from Nuvolari's Maserati in the Coppa Acerbo on 13th August. The following week-end Fagioli won again, this time the Comminges GP on the St Gaudens circuit in the valley of the Garonne in France.

Louis Chiron was now driving Alfa Romeos for the Scuderia Ferrari, and in the Marseilles GP he and Fagioli were first and second in P3s with Moll's Monza third. Nuvolari on the Maserati, by some poetic justice, retired with differential trouble.

The 10th September 1933 was one of the blackest days in motor racing history, when a triple tragedy occurred at Monza. In the morning the Italian GP was held on the old 10km circuit, which was being used for the last time, and Nuvolari's Maserati finished forty seconds behind Fagioli's P3, with Zehender's Maserati third ahead of six Monza Alfas in a row. Fagioli's record lap of 115.82mph compares with Ascari's record of 104.25mph with the P2 in 1924.

In the afternoon the Monza GP of three heats and a final was held on the Pista di Velocita, a true track race. Campari was back with Alfa Romeo driving a Monoposto with the front brakes removed, in the best tradition of the Brooklands outer circuit, and Borzacchini was driving the actual Maserati with which Campari had won the French GP. The first heat was won by Czaykowski's 4.9 Bugatti from Moll's and Bonetto's Monza Alfas (Moll's lap at over 122mph was fastest of the day), but during the race Count Trossi's Scuderia Ferrari single-seater Duesenberg threw a rod and spilled oil on the track. Whilst fighting for the lead at the beginning of the second heat, Campari and Borzacchini both skidded on the patch of oil, their cars left the track and Campari was killed

instantly, Borzacchini dying shortly afterwards. This tragedy was very deeply felt, for Campari was a well-loved figure, with his burly frame, huge enjoyment of good food and singing, excellent humour and natural simplicity and modesty: and he was the very epitome of Alfa Romeo racing, his experience going back further than that of any other Alfa driver. He left a widow, a well-known opera singer of the time, and a duaghter His house at San Siro, in Milan, Ferrari tells us, was so full of the paintings he had bought and the silver trophies which he had won that it was difficult to pick one's way between them. Borzacchini, too, who came from Terni, had left his mark in racing, and was so close to Nuvolari that he was affectionately referred to as Nuvolari's 'little brother'.

In the final of the Monza GP, the Polish Count Czaykowski also skidded on the oil patch on the South Curve and he, too, lost his life. The race was won by Lehoux's Type 51 Bugatti from Moll and Bonetto.

At the two remaining GP races of the 1933 season, Chiron and Fagioli in P3 Monopostos were first and second at Brno in the Czechoslovakian GP from Jean Pierre Wimille's 2.3 Monza Alfa and Dreyfus's 2.3 Bugatti, and they also headed the Spanish GP at San Sebastian from Lehoux (Type 51 Bugatti) and Varzi on one of the new Type 59 Bugattis, at that time with 2.8 litre engines.

The early 'thirties were the peak of Alfa Romeo fortunes in pre-war motor racing and have been examined in some detail because of this, and to show that motor racing some forty years ago could be almost as hectic as it is today, at any rate in the summer months. Admittedly the racing drivers of those days did not spend every winter racing on the other side of the world as is now the custom.

The decline in the fortunes of Alfa Romeo in motor racing until the time of the Second World War began gradually in 1934, and trends rather than details must suffice in tracing this decline.

CHANGING FORTUNES

1933 saw the last 6C 1750 Gran Sport built and effectively the last 8C 2300, for in 1934 only seven of the latter chassis were made.

One model replaced the 6C 1750, 6C 1900 and 8C 2300, its engine on the face of its being a mixture of the two previous designs, a six cylinder 2.3 litre. In fact it was a completely new engine, bearing little resemblance to its predecessors which were by way of being descended from the P2, whereas the new engine started another era in Alfa Romeo power units. The 6C 2300 as the new model was called was, perhaps, built down to a price more than the previous cars, the engine no longer having an alloy crankcase, but a cast iron one integral with the cylinder block. However, twin overhead camshafts were still featured, but driven from the front of the engine by gearwheels, bevels and a chain instead of a vertical shaft and bevel gears at the rear. Bore and stroke was 70 x 100mm, 2,309cc, and the power output of the Turismo model was 68bhp at 4,400rpm,

about the same as that of the smaller 6C 1900.

The chassis was boxed and very stiff, with semi-elliptic springs outboard of the chassis, as on the 8C 2300. The gearbox was similar to that on the 1900 with synchromesh on third and top and a freewheel, but the clutch was a single plate design. The torque tube final drive was the same as on the previous models.

The 6C 1900 and final 6C 1750 cars made in 1933 had been 6th Series, and it is interesting that the first 6C 2300 models were called 7th Series, so were evidently considered to be a direct follow-on of the earlier 6C cars.

There were three models, the 75mph Turismo, which had a long 10ft 6ins wheelbase and carried six or seven seater saloon coachwork by Castagna; the 80mph Gran Turismo, with a 9ft 7ins wheelbase, 76bhp engine, still with single carburettor, and four seater saloon coachwork by Carrozzeria Alfa; and finally the 90mph Pescara. This was a 95bhp twin carburettor version of the Gran Turismo with a higher compression ratio (7.75 to 1 instead of 6.75 to 1) fitted with ultra-light four seater closed bodywork by Touring of Milan. Three of these cars came first, second and third in the 1934 Targa Abruzzo 24 Hours Race at Pescara (hence the name) after all the 8C 2300 cars had retired. 225 Turismo cars were made, 473 Gran Turismo and 60 Pescaras, all in 1934. The 6C 2300 was a good car, though lacking the glamour of the supercharged 6C 1750 and 8C 2300.

The tendency for their rivals in Grand Prix racing to increase the size of their engines having been noted by Jano and Alfa Romeo, for 1934 they produced what was known as the Monoposto Type B 1934 (but still popularly known as the P3) of which the

In the 1934 French GP at Montlhery, Count Trossi handed this 2.9 litre Type B P3 over to Guy Moll after 14 laps with only two operative gears, and young Moll drove it to 3rd place in the 40 lap race

Mechanic working on the gearbox of Marcel Lehoux's P3 between heats at Dieppe in 1934, showing the unusual twin propeller shaft transmission which was peculiar to the P3 in GP racing

engine had an increase in bore from 65 to 68mm, so that the 68 x 100mm engine had a total capacity of 2,905cc. Power was now 255bhp at 5,400rpm and maximum speed over 160mph. The new Grand Prix rules demanded an unladen weight, not even including tyres, of not more than 750kg (14.73cwt) and a body width of not less than 33.5ins. Thus the P3 cockpits had to be broadened, and in the process the sides of the cockpit were raised somewhat.

Seven new cars were constructed in 1934, with enough spares for another four cars, and, in addition, older 2.6 litre cars were brought up to the new specification. Varzi, Chiron, Moll and Trossi were the main drivers for the season, with Brivio transferring from Bugatti later on.

At Monaco only Etancelin's 2.9 litre Maserati offered some sort of a challenge to the P3s, and Moll won from Chiron and Lehoux, who was in the Ferrari team for this race. Count Trossi put up fastest lap before retiring. The 2.8 litre Type 59 Bugattis seemed to lack acceleration and good brakes, and Nuvolari, who drove one in this race, then went back to Maseratis. At Avus the Alfas met the new German Auto Unions for the first time, but Moll managed to win in a special P3 with peculiar streamlined bodywork and a 3.2 litre engine. Alfa Romeo had called in an aircraft engineer to design the body, as had Mercedes for the aerodynamic SSKL which won at Avus in 1932. At the Eifel races on the Nurburg Ring Mercedes entered the fray with their sensational new cars, and the best P3, Chiron's, was third behind a Mercedes and an Auto Union. However, Chiron put up a wonderful performance at the French GP at Montlhéry in his P3, wearing down the German cars of Mercedes and Auto Union until they all retired, making fastest lap, and finishing in front of his team mates Varzi and Moll. This was the last occasion in 1934 that the P3 Alfas won against the German cars, though they sometimes managed to split them. Young Guy Moll, before he crashed and sadly lost his life in the 1934 Coppa Acerbo, actually made fastest lap in this last race of his by sheer driving ability against the Germans.

Although the P3s had little to worry about in races where the Germans were not present, even this situation began to change towards the end of 1934, by which time both the Type 59 Bugattis and the monoposto Maseratis were seen with bigger capacity engines of 3.3 litres. Nuvolari went back to the Bugatti team for just one race, the Spanish GP, in which he was third behind two Mercedes, then he drove a 3.3 litre Maserati, and beat the 2.9 P3 Alfas at both Modena and Naples.

Varzi on a 2.6 litre Monza Alfa won the Mille Miglia from Nuvolari on a 2.3 litre Monza which had been specially prepared by Jano and was as fast, but Varzi was helped by fitting special tyres which gave extra traction in the rain. Varzi also won the Targa Florio on a P3 Monoposto at 43mph, whilst Le Mans saw the last Alfa Romeo win to date, the car an 8C 2300 driven by Etancelin and Chinetti.

During 1935 the Scuderia Ferrari P3s were fitted with more powerful engines with bigger bores giving 3.2 litres, 3.5 litres and even 3.8 litres (78 x 100mm), power going up to 330bhp maximum. Strengthened gearboxes with only three speeds had to be installed, as the four speed boxes were not strong enough. Reversed quarter-elliptic springs replaced the half-elliptics at the rear at the beginning of the season, and later Dubonnet type

Louis Chiron, the French ace, at the wheel of a 3.8 litre P3 with Dubonnet independent front suspension at the 1935 Spanish GP at San Sebastian

Austin Dobson at Brooklands in the Bimotore with two 2.9 litre engines, one in front of the driver and one behind, which he acquired in 1937

independent front suspension and hydraulic brakes were also adopted. Nuvolari was back in the Ferrari team and had one great and memorable victory against the Germans with a 3.8 litre P3 in the German GP at the Nurnburg Ring. This race has been described countless times in motor racing histories.

In the Italian GP at Monza he appeared with a new 170mph Alfa Romeo, intended to have a twelve cylinder engine, but this was not ready until 1936, so the 3.8 litre eight cylinder engine was fitted in 1935, when the car was known as the 8C 1935, or 8C 35. It had all independent suspension by trailing links and coil springs in hydraulic dampers at the front and swing axles with a transverse leaf spring below the axle at the back, the gearbox being integral with the

back axle. Bodywork was rather bulbous, but the car was not unhandsome. In the Italian GP Nuvolari made fastest lap of the race when lying third in trying to catch up an Auto Union and a Mercedes, but broke a piston, and then took over Dreyfus's 3.8 litre P3 Monoposto and finished second to Stuck's Auto Union after all the Mercedes had retired. Nuvolari had seven victories in 1935 when the German cars were not present, mostly in 3.5 litre P3 cars at Nice, Pau, Leghorn, Modena, Turin and Biella, besides his classic German GP win.

A 6C 2300 in the hands of Cortese and Severi won the Targa Abruzzo again, and Brivio won the Targa Florio with a 2.9 litre P3 at 49.18mph, whilst Carlo Pintacuda and Della Stufa won the

Front view of the Bimotore. Built by the Scuderia Ferrari, it was the first car to carry the Ferrari shield as a radiator badge. The smooth tyres were fitted for Brooklands track racing

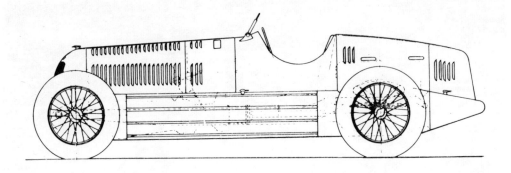

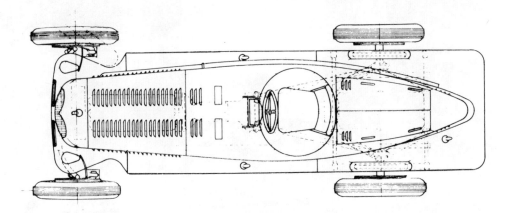

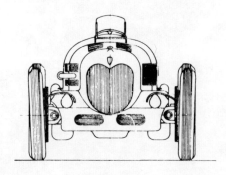

Bimotore drawing

Mille Miglia in a most unusual P3 converted into a two seater sports car with wings and lamps.

As an entirely Scuderia Ferrari venture, two Bi-Motore Alfa Romeos were built in less than four months at Modena in 1935, designed by Luigi Bazzi, and intended for formula libre races on very fast tracks and for record breaking. These cars each had a lengthened P3 chassis, with one P3 engine in the normal place, and the other in the tail behind the driver, who sat on top of the three speed gearbox between the engines. Front suspension was Dubonnet, the rear axle was jointed in the middle and located by radius rods, with semi-elliptic springs. One car built for Nuvolari had two 3.2 litre engines and the other built for Chiron had two 2.9 litre engines. The cars were raced in 1935 at Tripoli and Avus and proved to have an insatiable appetite for tyres, so they lost much time at the pits, whereas the Auto Unions and Mercedes did not have to make so many wheel changes. Nuvolari was fourth at Tripoli behind the Germans, and Chiron was second at Avus between Fagioli's Mercedes and Varzi's Auto Union.

In June 1935 Nuvolari broke the Class B (5,001-8,000cc) flying mile record with the 6.3 litre car on the Lucca to Altopascio stretch of the Florence-Viareggio autostrada. He averaged 200.8mph and fought the car for nearly two hundred yards on the outward run because of hitting a gust of wind after passing under an archway. On the return run he showed his courage by going even faster, but this time the car was not so badly affected by the crosswind.

In 1935 the 1st Series of the new 6C 2300B model was produced in Gran Turismo and Pescara form. Unusually, a Turismo version was the last to appear, in 1937. These cars had advanced all-independently sprung chassis, the front suspension being identical with that fitted to the 8C 35 GP car, by trailing links with coil springs in hydraulic dampers, but the rear swing axle suspension on the Porsche principle used torsion bars for springing instead of a transverse leaf. The gearbox on the 6C 2300B was integral with the engine instead of being part of the rear axle as on the racing car. The independently sprung cars had the same engines as the earlier 6C 2300 cars, which had semi-elliptics all round, but slightly longer chassis, the wheelbase being 9ft 10ins instead of 9ft 7ins for both the Gran Turismo and Pescara and not unnaturally they were somewhat heavier, by something approaching 2cwt. Again the saloon bodies on the Gran Turismo were by Alfa and those on the Pescara were by Touring, and these were quite pleasant to look at, being more streamlined than the rather square bodies on the previous series.

Finally, a sports car in the true Alfa Romeo tradition, only more so, was produced ready for the 1936 season known as the 8C 2900A. This was a sports/racing car, and the germ of the idea was probably the 'two seater' P3 which won the 1934 Mille Miglia, for the 8C 2900A looked like a two seater version of the 8C 35 GP car with cycle-type wings and two aero screens, and that is exactly what it was, though with a 2.9 litre engine. Only eleven cars were built, five in 1935, so they were very much 'works' cars.

It is of interest that the prototype of a small four cylinder version of the 6C 2300B intended for mass-production with an optional single or twin overhead camshaft engine and Alfa four seater saloon bodywork was evolved. Three examples of the Tipo 1 4C 1500 Prototipo were produced between 1935 and 1937, but the idea was abandoned.

During 1936 the new 4064cc V12 cylinder GP engine was ready and was put into the 8C 35 chassis, the car becoming known as the 12C 36. The 60 degree V12 engine gave 370bhp at 5,800rpm as opposed to the 330bhp at 5,400 of the 3,822cc eight cylinder, but performance was not all that superior to that of the smaller capacity car. External appearance was identical, except the twelve cylinder version had

Above: Nuvolari driving an 8C 35 GP car, distinguished by the outside
exhaust pipe on the offside
Below: A 12C 36 GP car, which had two exhaust pipes carried beneath the car

Above: 12C 36 engine
Below: An 8C 35 in the foreground and two 12C 36 cars in the background at
the 1937 German GP at the Nurburgring

two exhaust pipes running underneath the car instead of a single external pipe on the offside.

Although the 8C 35 and 12C 36 were slower and less powerful than the German cars in 1936, which definitely had the upper hand, particularly Auto Union, they enabled Nuvolari to put up some remarkable performances on the twistier circuits to prove the truth of Laurence Pomeroy's assertion that a brilliant driver in an inferior car can outclass a first class driver in a first class car. In fact if Berndt Rosemeyer had not been driving for Auto Unions, Nuvolari would have done even better than he did. To get the perspective right, Auto Union won at Tripoli, with Varzi driving, and then Rosemeyer won the Eifelrennen at Nurburg, the Hungarian GP at Budapest, the German GP at Nurburg, the Coppa Acerbo at Pescara, the Swiss GP at Berne and the Italian GP at Monza. Mercedes had a bad year, Caracciola winning for them only at Tunis and Monaco.

For about ten laps at Monaco Nuvolari's 8C 35 was in the lead ahead of Caracciola's Mercedes, a lead which built up to about ten seconds in pouring rain, then both his engine and brakes played up, and he finished fourth behind the Mercedes and two Auto Unions. In practice at Tripoli Nuvolari burst a tyre and turned his 12C 36 over, appearing in the race wearing a plaster corset, but he finished a lowly seventh, even behind his team mates.

In the Penya Rhin GP in Spain on 7th June over the twisting Montjuich Park circuit, Nuvolari on a 12C 36 had an absolute needle match with Caracciola's Mercedes and won by three seconds.

On the third lap of the German GP on the Nurburg Ring the following week-end Nuvolari's 12C 36 took the lead. At half distance Rosemeyer passed Nuvolari, and when banks of mist came rolling in over the circuit 'Nebelmeister' (Fog Master) Rosemeyer increased his lead and won from Nuvolari by two minutes.

On a twisty five kilometre circuit at Budapest, Nuvolari in an 8C 35 went into the lead in the Hungarian GP on 21st June, then was passed by Rosemeyer. On the thirty-fifth lap Nuvolari passed Rosemeyer in the tricky rear-engined Auto Union as he was coming out of a corner, and increased his lead to win the fifty lap race by fourteen seconds, thus turning the tables on the brilliant Berndt.

Just a week later in the Milan GP on a 1.6 mile circuit in the Sempione Park which included eight corners, two of which were hairpins, Nuvolari on a 12C 36 had a wheel-to-wheel duel with the single Auto Union entered, driven by Varzi, and won by nine seconds.

Nuvolari's most memorable race was the Coppa Ciano, in 1936 held over a long, fast yet tortuous circuit at Leghorn. Three Auto Unions, scarcely touched since the German GP the weekend before (in which Nuvolari retired his 12C 36) were entered and were hot favourites to win, particularly when Nuvolari fell out with his 12C 36 having back axle trouble shortly after the start. This incensed Nuvolari, who walked back to his pit and insisted on taking over another car. Carlo Pintacuda was the slowest of the team, in an 8C 35, so he was called in and Nuvolari set off in the car after the three Auto Unions in line ahead formation. With the spectators nearly weeping with excitement, Nuvolari not only caught up and passed the Auto Unions (drivers were Rosemeyer, Stuck and Varzi) but so demoralised them by causing them to wear out their brakes that they were also passed by Brivio and Dreyfus, respectively on 12C 36 and 8C 35 cars, thus giving Alfa Romeo a remarkable victory over Auto Union, the fastest cars in GP racing that year. This, and the 1935 German GP, were probably Nuvolari's greatest victories.

On the 23rd August, Nuvolari on a 12C 36 was second to Rosemeyer in the Swiss GP at Berne, then he went over to New York and easily won the Vanderbilt Cup on the Roosevelt Raceway, Long Island, in a 12C 36 from Wimille's Type 59 Bugatti, with Brivio's

The maestro Nuvolari at the Nurburgring in 1937 with Marinoni standing in the background wearing goggles

12C 36 third. On the way over to New York in the liner 'Rex', Nuvolari learned that his son Giorgio, who was in his late 'teens, had died from pericarditis following a bad bout of typhoid. By a melancholy coincidence Vittorio Jano, Enzo Ferrari and Guiseppe Merosi each suffered a similar tragedy in the loss of a son of about the same age as Giorgio Nuvolari, although for Jano and Ferrari this was still in the future.

Not surprisingly the 8C 2900A sports cars were difficult to beat in 1936, though they were nearly defeated in the Mille Miglia by Clemente Biondetti driving the converted P3 which had won the previous year, now fitted with a 3.2 litre engine. He was delayed, however, and finished fourth behind the three 8C 2900As of Brivio, Farina and Pintacuda, who finished in that order. Pintacuda and Marinoni raced two 2900As in Brazil in the summer of 1936 and were first and second in the Sao Paulo GP, whilst Sommer and Severi won the Belgian 24 Hour race

at Spa with an 8C 2900A at an average speed not beaten till 1949.

A curious feature of 1936, and a pointer to the relative unimportance of car production at that time in the Alfa Romeo works where items such as aircraft engines and armament work took precedence, was the fact that precisely ten cars were made during the year, five 8C 2900As and five 6C 2300B Pescara models. Thus passenger car production virtually ceased. This, of course, was the time of the Abyssinian crisis, when Italy was at war.

In 1937 the Turismo model of the 6C 2300B type was at last introduced for six seater Alfa saloon coachwork with the long wheelbase of 10ft 8ins. 78 cars were produced, all in 1937, and in this year 112 Pescaras were built, and 70 of the Gran Turismo type.

1937 also saw the introduction of the

A 1st Series 6C 2300B long chassis car with 6 seater bodywork, produced in 1936/7. All independent suspension was featured

production version of the 8C 2900A sports/racing car, known as the 8C 2900B. Only 30 were built, 20 in short chassis Spider two seater form with bodies by Touring or Pininfarina and 10 in long chassis four seater coupe form with bodies by Touring. The Corto (short) chassis had a wheelbase of 9ft 2ins compared to the 9ft of the 2900A, and the Lungo (long) chassis had a 9ft 10ins wheelbase. Engines were detuned to give 180bhp instead of the 220bhp of the 2900A, and as on the 2900A a Scintilla Vertex magneto was fitted. A 2900B in Mille Miglia form was brought up to 2900A tune and these Alfa Romeos were considered to be the fastest production pre-war cars in the world. Body styling varied from the beautiful to the comparatively hideous. 145mph was quoted as the maximum speed of the 2900A, 115mph for the 2900B Corto and 110mph for the Lungo. Today, a very large proportion of the surviving 2900B cars are in the United States.

The 1937 Mille Miglia was won by Carlo Pintacuda in an 8C 2900A Spider with an engine boosted to give 260bhp. A 3.5 litre French Delahaye was second.

The 6 hour Targa Abruzzo race at Pescara was won by Franco Cortese in a non-independently sprung 6C 2300, his third successive win in this race. He was destined to win in 1938, too, with a 6C 2300B.

Although the 8C 35 and 12C 36 GP cars continued to do well in Italian races, they were completely out-classed by the German cars in the major races. At Pescara in August, 1937, Jano's newest GP Alfa Romeo was entered by the works, not by the Scuderia Ferrari, for the Coppa Acerbo. These were beautiful looking low chassis cars, named 12C 37, fitted with an enlarged 4,495cc V12 engine. Unfortunately the roadholding was not right, and later when Guidotti's 12C 37 retired with back axle trouble in the Italian GP at Leghorn, Jano was blamed and was dismissed from Alfa Romeo as being 'too old'. In fact, with aircraft work taking priority, Jano had not had the opportunity to develop the car properly, and he was soon showing Alfa Romeo that he was far from being 'too old' by moving to Turin and producing some brilliant work for Lancia. This great designer died by his own hand in 1965 at the age of 74, under the mistaken impression that he

The 6C 2300B chassis with torsion bar rear independent suspension

The 6C 2300 saloon of 1934

was suffering from cancer.

In 1938 a new works-backed organisation called Alfa Corse took over the racing side of Alfa Romeo from the Scuderia Ferrari, though Enzo Ferrari himself was still in charge. Once again the 'quadrifoglio' returned to the racing cars in place of the Ferrari shield. Giaccomo Colombo, Jano's assistant with experience going back to the P2 days, was responsible for racing car design aided by Luigi Bazzi. Bruno Trevisan, who had been development designer for the twelve cylinder racing engine, was now designer of the production cars.

Some minor alterations were made to the 6C 2300B cars resulting in the 2nd Series. The Turismo was renamed the Lungo, the Gran Turismo the Corto and the Pescara became the Mille Miglia, but most noticeable was the fact that the Corto and Lungo now looked very mass-produced with pressed steel wheels, only the Mille Miglia retaining knock-on wire wheels. Total 1938 production was 542 cars; 270 had been made in 1937. The figure fell to

2nd Series 6C 2300B

372 cars in 1939, 29 Lungo and 13 Corto 6C 2300Bs and the rest 6C 2500s, of which more anon. Alfa Romeo prestige in those days was certainly not as a result of the volume of cars manufactured.

1938 saw the 3 litre GP formula come into being, and Alfa Corse fielded three types of car: the Type 312 (3 litres, 12 cylinders), which was the 3 litre version of Jano's low chassis 12C 37 in which the handling problems had been resolved, with a 320bhp, 2,995cc V12 engine; the Type 316, which had the same chassis with a 350bhp, 2,958cc V16 engine; and lastly the Type 308, which Fusi describes as the 8C 2900A

the most successful Alfa Corse GP driver in a poor season, coming second in the Coppa Ciano at Leghorn to Lang's Mercedes (Auto Unions were not running) driving a 312, where Wimille and Biondetti sharing a similar 312 finished in third place. In the Coppa Acerbo at Pescara, Farina was second to Caracciola's Mercedes in a 312, albeit over three minutes behind after the German cars had suffered many retirements. Farina drove a 316 in the Italian GP at Monza, and after two Auto Unions retired he finished second, $3\frac{1}{2}$ minutes after Nuvolari on the winning

Type 412 of 1939

converted into a single-seater, with the old straight eight engine bored out to 2,991cc from 2,905cc, and developing 295bhp at 6,000rpm. It goes without saying that all these engines were supercharged, and the V16 engine had twin crankshafts.

After his 8C 308 caught fire at the beginning of the season in practice for the 1938 Pau GP and caused him to crash, Nuvolari was very shaken and refused to race an Alfa Romeo again. He then went over to Auto Union to replace the incomparable Rosemeyer, who had been killed in a record breaking attempt.

In fact, Giuseppe ('Nino') Farina was

Auto Union, yet $7\frac{1}{2}$ minutes in front of the Mercedes shared by Caracciola and Brauchitsch. It must be confessed that Farina mainly succeeded by keeping on going when the faster German cars had stopped or were delayed.

The 2900B sports cars had a better season, Biondetti and Pintacuda coming first and second in the Mille Miglia, and Pintacuda and Severi winning the Belgian 24 Hours race. The sole Alfa Corse car at Le Mans, a 2900B coupé driven by Sommer and Biondetti, now to be seen at Lord Doune's motor museum at Doune in Perthshire, Scotland, retired late on the Sunday morning with a broken valve when it had a

Above : Production 2900A with Carrozzeria Alfa Spider bodywork
Below : 8C 2900B rear suspension

Above: The experimental low chassis 12C 37 GP car
Below: Farina practising for the Swiss GP at Berne in 1938 in a Type 312

Above: Dr Giuseppe Farina in a Type 316 in the 1938 Italian GP at Monza, in which he drove a fine race to finish second between Nuvolari's Auto Union and the Mercedes shared by Caracciola and von Brauchitsch
Below: The Frenchman Raymond Sommer in his hard worked Type 308 during the French GP at Rheims in 1939

lead of one hundred miles.

1938 was an important year in that it saw the first appearance of the Type 158 Alfa Romeo, or 'Alfetta'. With the German teams so dominant in Grand Prix racing aided by their large State subsidies, it seemed sensible for Alfa Corse to go in for 1½ litre voiturette racing which was mainly the province of the Italian Maseratis and the British ERAs. At least this class seemed safe from the German menace.

Colombo's 158 (1,500cc, 8 cylinders) was the first Alfa Romeo with a tubular chassis. It was mostly built at Modena, the straight eight engine was on the lines of its predecessors, but it had a single supercharger, and the camshafts and accessories were gear driven at the front of the engine. Originally the engine, with a bore and stroke of 58 x 70mm, 1,479cc, developed 195bhp at 7,200rpm, and the V16 engine in the Type 316 was, in fact, largely made up of 158 engine components, having the same bore and stroke. The 158 suspension was by swing axles and a transverse leaf spring at the rear like the earlier cars, but differed at the front by having trailing links using a transverse leaf spring instead of coil springs within dampers. The gearbox was mounted at the back of the car. The red single-seater 158s were very beautiful in appearance in their 1938 form, somewhat resembling the Type 308, but much better proportioned.

True to Alfa Romeo tradition, they won their first race, which took place before the Coppa Ciano at Leghorn, Emilio Villoresi being at the wheel, with another 158 driven by Clemente Biondetti coming second.

A fortnight later a similar voiturette race was a curtain raiser for the Coppa Acerbo at Pescara, but the 158s ran badly due to persistent plug trouble, and the race went to the Maseratis. Emilio Villoresi then won the Milan GP, a voiturette race before the Italian GP at Monza, one second ahead of his team mate Francesco Severi, but in the Circuit of Modena all the 158 cars retired.

Under Bruno Trevisan, who had been an aero engine designer with Fiat, the 6C 2300B cars were discontinued for 1939 and the 6C 2500 range substituted. These were similar to the earlier cars, with the same 100mm stroke, but the bore was increased from 70mm to 72mm, 2,443cc, and thus some more power was obtained. The six to seven seater saloon Turismo had a 10ft 8ins wheelbase, the five seater Sport saloon a 9ft 10ins wheelbase, while 8ft 8ins sufficed for the two seater Super Sport in open or closed form. With a three carburettor engine this model did 105mph. Spider two seater bodies were also available on the Sport chassis.

The most exciting car of the range was the 6C 2500SS Corsa, a light sports/racing car using the Super Sport chassis and having an engine tuned to give 125bhp at 4,800rpm instead of 110bhp. The Corsa was capable of 125mph.

The 8C 2900B was discontinued and Trevisan designed a big luxury car called the S10 to supplement the 2500, with five to six seater bodywork and a 3½ litre V12 engine. Only two prototypes were made. He also designed a 2.3 litre V8, the S11, which was intended to replace the 6C 2300B, but the 6C 2500B was decided upon instead, though two S11 prototypes were also built. In appearance the S10 Normale was a conventional and inoffensive saloon, but a drawing of the proposed S11 Normale looks quite nightmarish, like a cartoonist's exaggeration of an American style car of the time, but in the worst possible taste. Super Sport versions of both cars were visualised.

The old 8C 2900 tradition was continued in 1939 when a new sports/racing car was evolved from old components with the idea of possibly developing it into an unsupercharged 4½ litre for that category of Grand Prix racing. The engine was the V12 unit from the 12C 37, but with three downdraught Weber carburettors in place of the supercharger and the compression raised from 6.5 to 1 to 8.15 to 1.

Sommer/Biondetti 8C 2900B Coupe

It produced the same power, 220bhp at 5,500rpm as the supercharged 2.9 litre engine of the 8C 2900A had done at 5,300rpm. As this engine was put into the 8C 2900 chassis, the resultant car being known as the Type 412, the performance was similar, though possibly not quite up to 2900A standards

in some respects as the new car was heavier. Nevertheless, in the Antwerp GP sports car race in 1939, two Type 412s driven by Farina and Sommer dominated the Delage, Darracq and Delahaye opposition. After the war the Swiss Willy Daetwyler had hill climb and race successes with one of these cars.

In 1939 two 316 cars made an

them were six 158s, three works 4CL Maseratis, and twenty two other Maseratis, so the odds on an Italian success still seemed quite good. No sooner had the race started, however than all the works Maseratis promptly retired on the first lap while the two silver Mercedes were already in the lead. There was further consternation when the Mercedes went so fast that the 158s also began dropping out one by one with overheating. In the end Herman Lang won, Caracciola was second and the one remaining 158, Emilio Villoresi's, was third, the driver having had to deliberately keep his revs down in order to avoid overheating. Having enjoyed their little joke, the 1½ litre Mercedes then returned to Stuttgart and were never raced again.

As a result of this defeat, much redesigning went into the 158, and unfortunately in the course of the testing Emilio Villoresi lost his life at Monza. A change was made in the engine from plain to roller bearings for the crankshaft, the output was raised to 225bhp at 7,500rpm, and the appearance of the car was altered to the shape which became so well known post-war, the car losing some of its good looks in the process.

In this form the cars were unbeatable by the Maserati opposition in Italian races, and when a voiturette race was run concurrently with the 1939 Swiss GP at Berne, Farina's 158 was faster in the early stages than all the Auto Unions and all the Mercedes barring Lang's, though it dropped back to finish sixth, yet still in front of Stuck's Auto Union.

It has taken nine chapters to describe the first thirty years of Alfa Romeo history. The next thirty years have to be described in one chapter. This is because for some three-quarters of those thirty remaining years the main struggle was carried on in the industrial sphere rather than on the race tracks, though Alfa Romeo participation in sporting competitions has never ceased, and seems unlikely to do so.

appearance in the Belgian GP at Spa, Biondetti retiring, but Farina finishing fourth behind two Mercedes and an Auto Union, which was second.

All the major Italian races in 1939 were for 1½ litre voiturettes, so an Italian victory seemed assured. Suddenly, to every loyal Italian's horror, Mercedes appeared at Tripoli with two new 1½ litre V8 cars. To oppose

SATTA'S SAGA

In 1936 an unusual Spanish engineer had come to join the Alfa Romeo design staff called Wilfredo Ricart, then thirty eight years old. In Spain he had designed sports and racing cars and diesel engines, had organised the public transport and omnibus services in Valencia, and he also held a pilot's licence. From 1940 until he left the firm in 1945, subsequently to design the Spanish Pegaso car, he was in charge of design at Alfa Romeo.

Enzo Ferrari made no secret of disliking him and, in fact, his appointment led to Ferrari leaving Alfa Romeo. Ricart had a habit of wearing shoes with enormously thick rubber soles, and when Ferrari one day asked him why he affected these, Ricart replied, with apparent seriousness, that a great engineer's brain must be carefully sprung against the inequalities of the ground in case its delicate mechanism is disturbed.

The rubber suspended brain was busy during the war years, though it must be admitted on projects which were not followed through, as none got past the prototype stage. One of these was a 2,000hp aero engine with what might be thought a record number of cylinders for any internal combustion engine – twenty-eight, in seven rows of four, though Gabriel Voisin designed a forty-two cylinder aero engine in 1939, in six banks of seven, also of 2,000hp.

In the car field, in 1939, Ricart worked on the Type 162, a V16 3 litre Grand Prix car, from which 490bhp at 7,800rpm was claimed and 560bhp at 8,200rpm anticipated. The roller bearing engine had sixty four valves, five superchargers (two high pressure, two low pressure, each three lobe Roots type, plus one centrifugal) and two carburettors. It is a surprise to find that the gearbox only boasted a modest four speeds. The tubular chassis had De Dion rear suspension. Parts for six cars were made, but only one was

Comm Dr Ing Orazio Satta, who has been responsible for Alfa Romeo design for a quarter of a century

**The 6C 2500 Coloniale model of
1939–1942**

assembled. This was tested in June
1940, but was abandoned when Italy
entered the war.

Ricart's next design, an example of
which is still in existence, was the rear-
engined Type 512 GP car with a flat
twelve cylinder centrifugally supercharged engine, giving 335bhp at
8,600rpm from 1,490cc. Parts for three
cars were made and two examples were
built. They were said to handle badly
and, in fact, the popular Attilio Marinoni
was killed in 1940 whilst testing a 512
on the Milan-Varese autostrada.

In 1941 Ricart came out with the Type
163, which had the Type 162 engine in
unsupercharged 190bhp form with
eight carburettors, and was a two seater
closed bodied rear engined sports/
racing car. It was really a mixture of

**The 6C 2500 Sport with 'Freccia
d'oro' Superleggera coachwork
by Carrozzeria Touring 1947**

132

the Type 163 engine and the Type 512 chassis using parts from each, and only one chassis was built, the bodywork never being completed.

Finally, in 1943, Ricart produced a six seater saloon, intended to be the first post-war production Alfa Romeo. Known as the 6C 2000 'Gazzella', this had an 85bhp, 1,954cc, twin overhead camshaft engine with single carburettor and coil ignition in a body and chassis of integral construction, with torsion bar independent suspension all round, and the gearbox in the rear axle. Maximum speed was 95–100mph. It was successfully tested immediately after the war was over, but such was the devastation at Portello due to the bombing, it was decided it would not be economic to go into production, and the 6C 2500 was continued instead.

What is rather surprising is the number of Sport and Super Sport Alfa Romeos which were turned out during the war years, quite apart from the Coloniale, a 6C 2500 Army vehicle, of

Biondetti and the 8C 2900B Alfa Romeo belonging to Romano with which they won the 1947 Mille Miglia

which a total of 152 were made. The figures are 83 Coloniale and 4 6C 2500 Sport in 1941, 67 Coloniale, 53 Sport and 12 Super Sport in 1942 53 Turismo, 24 Sport and 16 Super Sport in 1943, and 18 Sport in 1944. In 1945 only 6 Turismo and 3 Sport cars were made, but production went up in 1945 to 80 Turismo, 68 Sport and 17 Super Sport.

By 1943 the Design Department had been evacuated from Milan to the village of Melzo, in the countryside around Lake Orta, and the Gazella was designed there. When the Germans took over control of Northern Italy in 1943, the seven Type 158s in existence together with the two 512s were laid up in garages at Monza. The Germans used Monza as a vehicle park, but before they moved in the Secretary of the Milan Automobile Club had seen that the racing cars were moved away

to the rural retreat of the Design Department, where it is said they were hidden in a cheese factory.

In 1940 the modified 158s had again run at Tripoli, this time with no German opposition, and there was satisfaction in the fact that Farina in the winning car averaged 5mph more than Lang's 1½ litre Mercedes had in 1939, and beat the Mercedes fastest lap by 1.02mph.

The two most successful Alfa Romeo types in post war racing up to 1951 'were the works entered 158 1½ litre in Grand Prix races and the 3 litre 308 in private hands in formula libre. In 1946 the 158 had three wins, and the 308 two wins, the latter being in France in the hands of Jean Pierre Wimille in the Perpignan GP and the Bourgogne GP at Dijon.

The first appearance of the revived 158s was in June 1946, for the St Cloud GP near Paris, where both Farina and Wimille retired with seized clutch bearings due to overheating through being much used on the twisty circuit. At Geneva for the GP des Nations in

July, Farina and Wimille were joined in the team by Varzi and Trossi. Farina and Varzi, and possibly Wimille, had cars with two-stage superchargers and twin exhaust pipes giving 254bhp at 7,500rpm and known as Type 158/46B. Wimille made fastest lap in this two heats and a final event, and Farina won the final from Trossi, Wimille and Nuvolari on a 4CL Maserati. Nuvolari had his last big race win with this Maserati at Albi that year before contracting an ailment from which he eventually died in 1953, soon after his sixtieth birthday.

For the Turin GP in Valentino Park, five 158/46Bs took part, the new driver being Consalvo Sanesi, the chief mechanic and head tester from the factory. Farina and Sanesi retired with transmission trouble, and Wimille made fastest lap, but had to let Varzi win by half a second under team orders. Wimille had a disagreement with Alfa Romeo, probably as a result of this, so did not appear in the team for the Milan GP in the Parco Sempione, in which Trossi won the final from Varzi and Sanesi. Nuvolari on his Maserati had been third behind the Alfas in the first heat, but had to retire on the third lap of the final, too ill to carry on.

Early in 1947 Varzi went out to the Argentine and won two races in a Type 308, this model really coming into its own after the war, whereas before the war the works looked upon it as something of a stop-gap until the 312 and 316 cars were ready. It was always a good proposition for private owners, however, and Sommer had raced one successfully in 1939.

In 1947 development on the 158/46B two stage supercharged engines brought the output up to 275bhp, still at the same revs of 7,500rpm. Farina left the team until 1950, but Wimille returned to the fold, and won the first race of the season, the two heats and a final Swiss GP from Varzi and Trossi. The same order resulted in the European GP at Spa, where neither Sommer's 4CL Maserati or Chiron's 4½ litre unblown Lago Talbot were in any way a menace to the Alfas.

In the Bari GP only Varzi and Sanesi were entered, and Varzi had such an easy victory over the Maseratis that he was able to wait for Sanesi after he had spun on a corner and stalled his engine, so that the two of them could cross the line within three seconds of each other. In the Italian GP on the site of the Milan Fair a Portello mechanic, Alessandro Gaboardi, replaced Wimille, and drove sensibly in his only race to finish fourth behind Trossi, Varzi and Sanesi, albeit five laps behind the leader. To show the finish was prearranged, Trossi drove across the line with his goggles up and hands off the wheel.

In this year it was found that the increase in engine power caused small cracks in the electron crankcases near the main bearings, so the main bearing caps had tie rods fitted round them attached to the cylinder blocks, and this apparent jury-rig lasted the racing life of the cars.

Early in 1948 Varzi was off to the Argentine again, where he was tremendously popular, and was hoping to make his home when he retired from racing. In fact he formed the 'Scuderia Achille Varzi', which helped to further Juan Manuel Fangio's career in racing. In 1948 Varzi drove an interesting car in South America, a 12C 312 with the V12 engine enlarged to 4.6 litres, and won the Argentine Mar del Plata GP with it, whilst Jean Pierre Wimille won the Brazilian Sao Paulo GP with his old 308, and the Brazilian Chico Landi had two wins in 1948 Argentina races with a 308.

In 1947 a more powerful 158 was developed, but not actually raced, called the 158/47. This incorporated a larger low-pressure blower which increased the power output to 310bhp, still at 7,500rpm, and one or two other detail alterations were made, the most noticeable being a return to the single exhaust pipe.

While testing one of these cars in the wet on the Bremgarten Circuit before the 1948 Swiss GP, Varzi had one of

A Type 158 'Alfetta' in its post-war form

the rare accidents in his career and was killed. His faithful mechanic, Amedeo Bignami, who was to Varzi as Decimo Campagnoni was to Nuvolari, joined Fangio after Varzi's death, and accompanied the Argentine driver for most of his career.

The new San Remo 4CLT/48 tubular chassis Maserati appeared at Berne, but it was safe Alfa victory, for Trossi won from Wimille with Luigi Villoresi's San Remo Maserati third and Sanesi fourth. The 158/47 was not raced at Berne, nor was it in the French GP at Rheims, where a nice touch was the one appearance in the team of Antonio Ascari's son, Alberto. Wimille won by twenty-five seconds from Sanesi and Ascari, the latter driving on team orders and crossing the line half a second behind Sanesi.

The 1948 Italian GP in Turin's Valentino Park saw the first appearance of the Colombo designed V12 super-

charged 1½ litre Ferraris driven by Sommer, Farina and Bira, in addition to the San Remo Maseratis. Wimille won in a 158/47, making its debut in a race, but the older 158s had trouble, Sanesi retiring with a bent front axle and Trossi with supercharger trouble.

In October 1948, Monza was at last reopened, and in the 312 mile Monza GP Wimille, Trossi and Sanesi had single exhaust 158/47s and a new member of the team, Piero Taruffi, had an older single-exhaust car, this being the order in which they finished the race ahead of Maserati, Talbot, Ferrari and ERA opposition.

1949 opened tragically with the death of Jean Pierre Wimille while practising in a little Simca-Gordini for a race in Buenos Aires, and then the charming and witty pipe-smoking anglophile, Count Felice Trossi, died in bed of cancer. Partly because of this and because they were busy with the new 1900 production model, Alfa Romeo retired from racing in 1949.

A return was made in 1950 and some

work on the engine induction system produced the 158/50 model, which now gave 350bhp at 8,600rpm. Fangio, Farina and Fagioli were engaged as the main drivers, a fourth car sometimes being offered to a prominent driver from whichever country the team happened to be racing in.

Fangio started the season driving a lone 158/50 at San Remo against numerous supercharged 1½ litre V12 Ferraris, and successfully vanquished them. In the Grand Prix de l'Europe at Silverstone before the British Royal Family no Ferraris were entered, and the Alfa Romeos won as they liked, the finishing order being Farina, Fagioli, and the British driver Reg Parnell. Fangio retired with a broken connecting-rod, and the next car, a French Talbot, finished two laps in arrears of the Alfas.

At Monaco Fangio made fastest lap and won from Ascari's Ferrari and Chiron's Maserati, Fagioli and Farina having been eliminated in a multiple accident, and in the Swiss GP at Berne

Farina won by a fraction of a second from Fagioli, while Fangio retired with valve trouble. All the Ferraris retired and a Talbot was third.

There was a straw in the wind in the Belgian GP at Spa, where Ascari was driving an unblown 3.3 litre V12 Ferrari with a new engine designed by Lampredi, but the Alfas won again, Fangio this time, with Fagioli again second and Farina fourth behind Rosier's Talbot after being delayed by gearbox troubles.

At Rheims for the French GP Fangio broke Lang's 3 litre Mercedes lap record in practice and won the race from Fagioli after the Ferraris had scratched, and at Bari, where the Ferraris also did not appear, Farina won from Fangio.

For the GP des Nations at Geneva, Taruffi replaced Fagioli in the team, and the fourth car was given to the Swiss driver Baron de Graffenreid. This time Villoresi drove the 3.3. litre Ferrari and Ascari had a 4.1 litre version producing 310bhp, and these cars went fast enough in practice to make the front row of the grid. In the race only Fangio kept ahead of Ascari, then Villoresi crashed and Farina, too, in avoiding him. Ascari retired with water coming from his exhaust pipe, as it had done from the exhaust of his father's P2 at Lyons in 1924, and the finishing order was Fangio, de Graffenreid, and Taruffi, Taruffi doing well by putting up fastest lap.

After wins by Fangio in the Coppa Acerbo at Pescara and by Farina in the International Trophy at Silverstone, there came the Italian GP at Monza in September, where Taruffi and Sanesi joined 'the three Fs' to make a five car Alfa team, and Ascari and Serafini drove V12 Ferraris now enlarged to 4.5 litres. Fangio and Farina had 159 Alfas giving 370bhp and Farina won the race and became the first World Champion driver, also giving the Alfas their eleventh win in a season of eleven starts. Ascari, however, led the race for two laps in his Ferrari before retiring, and then took over Serafini's

Berne, 1948 where these 158 Alfa Romeos driven by Trossi, Wimille and Sanesi were first, second and fourth, with Villoresi's San Remo Maserati third.

car to finish second to Farina with Fagioli third, seventeen seconds behind.

For 1951 yet more power was squeezed out of the basically thirteen year old Alfa engine, and four brand new cars were built for the season with extra tanks to cope with the 1.6mpg fuel consumption now demanded by the engine giving well over 400bhp at 9,000rpm. De Dion back axles were also fitted.

During 1951 the 159s ran in non-Championship meetings at Silverstone, Dundrod, for the Ulster Trophy, and Goodwood where they easily showed their superiority, but in the Championship races they really were up against it for the first time, the new 4.5 litre Ferraris with twenty-four plug heads being a real worry.

At Berne for the Swiss GP Taruffi replaced Ascari, who had burned his arm, in the Ferrari team and finished second to Fangio; at Spa the Alfas were still obviously faster, particularly when they had burned off some of their fuel load, and Farina won from Ascari, despite making two pit stops for fuel to the Ferrari's one over 315 miles; in the French GP at Rheims the Ferraris had reshaped bodies and were faster, but Fangio won from Ascari after both had swapped cars with their team mates.

The crunch came in the British GP at Silverstone in July, where the Argentine driver Froilan Gonzalez drove an older twelve plug head Ferrari and did the first 100mph lap of the circuit in practice which the Alfas were unable to equal. In the race a tremendous duel took place between Fangio and Gonzalez, but Gonzalez won by fifty-one seconds, and the Alfettas were beaten for the first time since St Cloud in 1946.

In the German GP at the Nurburg Ring there was another Ferrari victory, where Ascari won from Fangio.

The Alfas for the Italian GP were designated 159M – 'M' for 'Maggiorata' or 'increased' – meaning they were stretched to their limit in every respect. They even had two exhaust pipes again, plus De Dion rear axles. Three of the four cars were so stretched they retired, and only Farina was left in vain pursuit of Ascari and Gonzalez, touching 9,000rpm and delayed by poor Alfa pitwork, which was not up to the Ferrari standard.

The culminating point in the Alfa Romeo/Ferrari battle was the Spanish GP over the Pedralbes Circuit at Barcelona in October, for each had now won three victories. In the race the Ferraris were delayed by tyre troubles and Fangio won with Gonzalez second, Farina third and Ascari fourth, Fangio also winning the World Championship.

This was the last great Alfa Romeo victory in racing, for the Portello firm thenceforth retired from Grand Prix racing. Due to the circumstances which prevailed at the time as a result of the war, the 158/9 Alfa Romeo was the most successful Grand Prix car ever built as it had more Grande Epreuve victories to its credit than any one model had ever achieved before or is, perhaps, likely to achieve again.

Orazio Satta was born in Turin on 6th October, 1910. After graduating at the Polytechnic in Turin in 1933 he did his military service and then qualified in aeronautical engineering in 1935. For the next three years he was deputy chief of the Aeronautical Laboratory of the Turin Polytechnic then, in 1938, he joined Alfa Romeo in the Special Projects and Experimental Department. In 1946 he took charge of Alfa Romeo design, and therefore has guided progress from the conversion of the Type 158 from single-stage to two-stage supercharging, as well as the building of the 159, to successive touring, sports and sports/racing Alfa Romeos up to this day. Just three people have substantially guided Alfa

Juan Manuel Fangio, 1951 World Champion, winning the 1951 Swiss Swiss GP at Berne in a Type 159

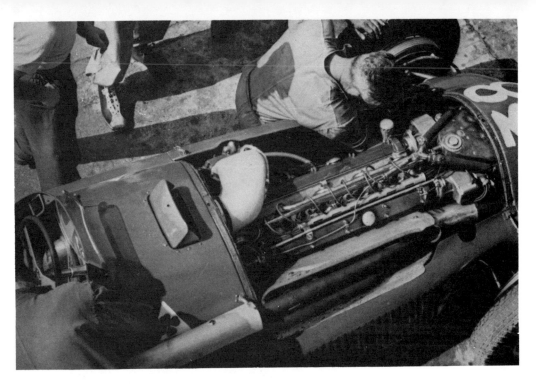

Above: The 159 engine in its final form developed over 400bhp from $1\frac{1}{2}$ litres, and did about $1\frac{1}{2}$ miles to the gallon of fuel
Below: Barcelona 1951. The Swiss Baron de Graffenreid in the Type 159 nearest the camera steals a glance at Ascari's V12 $4\frac{1}{2}$ litre Ferrari, the model which finally defeated the victorious Alfettas

Its big tyres are a noticeable feature of the 6C 2500 Super Sport of 1952

Romeo design over six decades, Merosi, Jano and Satta, and of the three it is of interest that only Satta had academic qualifications in engineering, Jano never bothered about them, and his title of Ingegnere (Engineer) was an honorary one, while, as we have seen, Merosi was a qualified surveyor.

After the war it was decided to concentrate on 6C 2500 production. The only new model was the 'Freccia d'Oro' or 'Golden Arrow', incorporating new and quite shapely mildly aerodynamic five/six seater bodywork by Carozzeria Alfa on the Sport chassis. Less 'Sport' in conception was its gear lever on the steering column, but then the long gear lever sprouting out of the floor which it replaced was nothing to write home about either. Coupe and saloon bodies, mostly by Touring, were also available on this chassis, and the seventeen-inch perforated disc wheels always looked huge,

presumably because they were shod with 6.50 section tyres.

The Mille Miglia was got going again in 1947 over a long 1,130 mile course starting at Brescia as usual, but then going clockwise down the Adriatic coast to Pesaro, across to Rome then to Leghorn, Florence, Turin, Milan and to finish at Brescia. Ln 1940 the Mille Miglia had been a utility affair over nine laps of a one-hundred mile circuit, Brescia-Cremona-Mantua-Brescia and a 2 litre BMW won from the Farina/Mambelli 6C 2500 Alfa Romeo.

In the 1948 Mille Miglia there was no official Alfa Romeo team, superchargers were banned, and Nuvolari had an heroic drive in an open 1,100cc Cisitalia, heading a race which finished in torrential rain. Nuvolari was pursued by Biondetti in an 8C 2900 fixed head coupe, with supercharger removed, a raised compression and four Solex carburettors. Nuvolari's ignition was swamped in the rains, and Biondetti had fuel feed difficulties and lost the use of first and second gears. Nevertheless, he made up time on the fast roads in the north and finished fifteen minutes ahead of Nuvolari, who came second and was so ill he had to be lifted out of his car at Brescia. Biondetti's car belonged to his co-driver Romano, and had been the 1938 Paris Salon show car. Today it belongs to Lucio Bollaert in Buenos Aires who runs it supercharged again.

Three 6C 2500 Competizione sports/racing two seater coupes were built with a transverse leaf spring replacing the standard torsion bars at the rear. In comparison with the 1939 6C 2500SS Corsa they had 9.2 to 1 instead of 8 to 1 compression ratios and gave 149bhp at 5,500rpm instead of 125bhp at 4,800rpm. They also had a shorter wheelbase and were lighter, though maximum speed of 125mph was about the same. It was with one of these cars that Franco Rol was third in the 1949 Mille Miglia to two Type 166 Ferraris,

The 2 litre Disco Volante Spider of 1952

and second to a similar car in the Targa Florio, Biondetti being the winning driver on each occasion. Rol managed to beat a Ferrari to first place in the Circuit of Pescara, run in heavy rain.

In 1950 Sanesi won the two hour Inter-Europa Cup sports car race at Monza in a similar Competizione coupe ahead of Lance Macklin's Aston Martin. In the 1950 Mille Miglia Sanesi drove a coupe with a 2,955cc engine called the 6C 3000 C50, but crashed after hitting a bump and striking his head on the low roof. Fangio, Rol and Bonetto had normal coupes with $2\frac{1}{2}$ litre engines, and Fangio finished third behind the 3.3 litre Ferraris of Marzotto and Serafini after his passenger, Zanardi, had also banged his head on the roof when Fangio hit a gulley at 112mph.

Sanesi's car had an engine developing 168bhp, but a touring prototype saloon with the same engine was built in detuned form giving 120bhp and called the 6C 3000. This was abandoned in favour of the 1900, which succeeded the 6C 2500.

6C 2500 production had reached a peak of 486 cars in 1947, followed by 451 in 1948 and 414 in 1949. With the 1900, Alfa Romeo seriously entered the mass production field for the first time. This model was introduced in 1950, and had a pressed steel integral body and chassis, front suspension by double wishbones and coil springs, and independent suspension was abandoned at the back, being replaced by a well located solid back axle on coil springs with telescopic dampers. The engine had chain driven twin overhead camshafts and was the first production four cylinder Alfa Romeo since Merosi's RMU. Cylinder dimensions were 82.55 x 88mm, 1,884cc, and power was 80bhp at 4,800rpm with a single Solex car-

Fangio in the 6C 3000 CM Disco Volante Coupe during his classic drive in the 1953 Mille Miglia in which he finished second with his steering operating on only one front wheel

The 1900 Sprint with a Coupe body by Touring was built from 1951–53 and the 1900 was the first mass-produced Alfa Romeo

burettor and 93bhp at 5,300rpm with a twin-choke Weber, giving 90mph and 105mph respectively.

In 1951 the 1900/C was produced with coupe or cabriolet coachwork, and a 100bhp engine. This engine in the saloon chassis became the 105mph 1900 TI (Turismo Internationale), and with the bore increased to 84.5mm and a total capacity of 1,975cc, a 115bhp engine in the saloon became the 110mph 1900 TI Super. The steering wheel was on the left in the 1900 series, and in the peak years of 1952–1954 annual production averaged 4500 units. The cars were not cheap for mass-produced saloons, a basic £1,300 in England for the cheapest model, but the performance was particularly good.

The TI saloons did well in touring car races, but an attempt at domination of the sports/racing field was made in 1953, resulting in the Disco Volante (Flying Saucer) cars, so called because of the shape of their original bodywork. These had special tubular chassis and could be had in 2 litre four cylinder form with an engine developed from the 1900, or in 260bhp six cylinder $3\frac{1}{2}$ litre form with a De Dion rear axle and an engine developed from the 3 litre that had appeared in the proto-type saloon and the coupe Sanesi drove in the Mille Miglia that year.

In the 1953 Mille Miglia, Fangio, Karl Kling and Sanesi drove $3\frac{1}{2}$ litre six cylinder coupés and Zehender a 2 litre four cylinder. After leading the race against Ferrari opposition, first Sanesi and then Kling retired and Zehender was also out of the race. Fangio was in the lead at Florence and then had a big drama when he found that only the right front wheel was answering to the steering. Despite this

The Giulietta Sprint Special with Bertone body was produced from 1960 to 1962

he pressed on, having to slow drastically to get round corners in the Appenines, where he was passed by Marzotto's 4.1 litre Ferrari, but averaged over 100mph on the straight roads between Bologna and Brescia to finish second to Marzotto at over 85mph – a famous drive in Fangio's career.

Three big Disco Volantes were entered for Le Mans in 1953, but they all retired, and a single car driven by Fangio and Sanesi retired early on in the 24 Hours race at Spa when Sanesi had a minor accident. After Kling's steering broke in practice for the 1,000 Kilometres Sports Car Race at the Nurburg Ring, the entire team was withdrawn. Finally Fangio drove an open version in the 1953 GP of Supercortmaggiore at Merano in September, and won against Ferrari, Lancia and Maserati opposition. This was the last

The Giulia TZ (Tubolare Zagato) of 1963 was a competition car with independent rear suspension

The 2000 Spider of 1958–61 was distinguished by the two air intakes on top of the bonnet

Disco Volante appearance in racing.

In 1954 the famous little four cylinder 74 x 75mm, 1,290cc, Giulietta model was introduced in which the traditional Alfa Romeo method of valve adjustment was abandoned, and shims were used instead on the twin ohc engine. The first Giulietta was an 80bhp Bertone two seater coupe, known as the Sprint. In 1955 came the 53bhp saloon and the open version of the Sprint called the Spider. In 1956 the Sprint and Spider Veloce had 90bhp engines, whilst the five speed gearbox Sprint Speciale in 1960 had a 100bhp engine. Annual Giulietta production was over 35,000 by 1961. A well located solid back axle was still retained. In 1958 the 2000 in saloon and Spider form replaced the 1900, and itself was replaced by the 2600 in 1952 when the 78 x 82mm, 1,570cc, Giulia series were brought

Above : Spider Duetto bodywork by Pininfarina
Below : The Giulia 1300 TI was the smallest Alfa Romeo saloon on the market in 1970
Right : The Giulia GTC Cabriolet was first seen in 1965

into being. From 1959 Alfa Romeo commenced making the Renault Dauphine in Italy under license.

The Portello works being in a residential area, further expansion was not possible, so in 1961 the construction of a new factory was started out at Arese, about ten miles from Portello, and this is now in operation with a capacity to produce 150,000 vehicles a year. The now well known Giulia Sprint GT with attractive coupé bodywork not so rounded as that on previous models was first introduced at Arese in 1963. An Alfa Romeo test track has also been built at Balocco, some forty-three miles west of Milan.

In 1968 a further stretched version of the original Giulietta engine appeared in a slightly larger body/chassis than the Giulia's and was called the 1750 in honour of the famous model of the past, of which a Giulia based 'replica' had been brought out in 1965. Known as the GS 4R Zagato, this 'replica' bore a somewhat superficial resemblance to the Vintage original, but was a good 'fun car'.

With the appearance of the 1750 the 2600 was dropped.

The Alfa Romeo range today embraces the best of all worlds, every model having a five speed gearbox and disc brakes. The range includes the 1300 Giulia TI saloon, 1600 Giulia Super saloon and 1750 saloon, the Giulietta name having been dropped for the smallest model, and the 116mph, 110mph, Super saloon being the survivor of the original 1,600cc engined Giulia series. In addition, the 1300 and 1750 are available in closed coupé form as the 103bhp, 105mph, Giulia 1300 2+2 and the 132bhp, 118mph, 1750 GT Veloce 2+2, also as open two seaters, the 1300 Spider and 1750 Spider Veloce. The saloons and coupés are Bertone designs, and the 'Duetto' Spiders are by Pininfarina.

The British magazine 'Autocar' summed up the new 1750 saloon in 1968

A 1750 GT-Am in the 4 hours of Jarama race in Spain 1970

very succinctly in the following words: 'Excellent performance. Sweet gearchange. Good quiet ride. Superb steering, handling and roadholding. Potent servo brakes. Lacks legroom for tall drivers. Very refined car and still an Alfa. Expensive in Britain.'

On test they reached 116mph, with a 0–60mph figure of 10.8 seconds, and 26mpg. Total price, with tax, in 1970 was £1,935.

In 1964, on a small trading estate about a mile outside Milan, the successor to the Scuderia Ferrari and Alfa Corse was founded, known as Autodelta, with Ing Carlo Chiti in charge. Chiti, described by Ferrari as 'a man of vast theoretical knowledge equalled only by his eagerness to win a reputation for himself' had been with Alfa Romeo from 1952 to 1957, and then until 1961 was chief engineer to the Ferrari racing team, subsequently going to ATS.

Autodelta's job at present is to develop and race touring, sports and sports prototype Alfa Romeos. At first, in 1965 and 1966, many class successes were obtained with the attractive little Giulia TZ (Tubolare Zagato) coupes, lightweight cars of which only 120 were built from 1963, 10 with fibreglass bodies. Later, from 1965, the lower TZ2 was raced with a twin plug cylinder head engine. All these TZ cars were unusual in having independent rear suspension.

Although 1300s were also used, the mainstay of Autodelta racing since 1966 has been the GTA coupe, 'A' standing for 'Allegerita' ('Lightened'), a lightweight version of the Giulia Sprint GT coupé, also fitted with a twin plug head. For Group 5 Special Touring Car races, superchargers were fitted, also fibreglass bodies. The European Touring Car Challenge Cup fell to GTAs in 1966 and 1967, when Andrea de Adamich won the TT at Oulton Park.

In 1970 the 2 litre GTAm was very successful in touring car races, the Am standing for America, for which market these cars were homologated, fitted with slightly enlarged 1750 engines

The 1970 'Montreal'

plus fuel injection. The GT 1300 also did well in such races, and by the end of the summer Alfa Romeo were firmly in the lead for the European Touring Car Challenge, and also won the under 2 litre class of the 1970 Trans-American Championship.

In 1967 a sports/racing prototype was announced, the Type 33, designed by Orazio Satta and 'the stubborn and able' Giuseppe Busso, to quote Ferrari again. This was a real racing car, having no affinities with the production range, at first with a 2 litre V8 engine set amidships in a twin-tube chassis and raced in both open and closed form. For 1969 a normal platform chassis with boxed alloy side members replaced the twin-tube structure, and $2\frac{1}{2}$ and subsequently 3 litre engines were developed. The cars have not been trouble-free, and though several class wins and one or two outright wins had been obtained by 1970, the car had yet to prove any marked superiority over its rivals, Nevertheless, some good performances were put up in 1970, and it was a better year than 1969. 424bhp was claimed from the 3 litre engine of the 33/3.

This engine was also fitted to a Formula 1 McLaren driven by Andrea de Adamich throughout 1970 in the major GP races as a McLaren team

member. The 'McAlfa' was not really competitive, but as it seemed to show promise, the project was persevered with throughout the season, though abandoned for 1971.

At the 1967 Montreal 'Expo' Exhibition, a special coupé based on the Type 33 was shown as a styling exercise by Bertone, and two years later the front-engined 'Montreal' model with a solid rear axle and a four overhead camshaft 2.6 litre fuel injection V8 engine was exhibited at the Geneva Show and was available to special order. It is rumoured that if a bigger production model is made to replace the 2600, it will have a V8 engine.

As to the future, a big project known as Alfa Sud is taking shape just outside Naples, Nicola Romeo's birthplace, where the aviation side of Alfa Romeo has traditionally been situated. While a new factory is being built here, the evaluation is going on of a small high performance saloon – rumoured to have front-wheel-drive and a 1 litre engine – which will be in production by 1972.

With the concentration at Alfa Sud on a single model, it is expected very large numbers will be produced at low cost, so it may not be long before we shall all be able to afford an Alfa Romeo.

The Author
Peter Hull

Born 1921, educated Dulwich College. Served London Scottish Regt. 1939–41 and in the R.A.F. 1941–46 and 1953–65 as a flying instructor on light aircraft and jets. Now Assistant Secretary of the Vintage Sports-Car Club. Author of several motoring books including *Alfa Romeo – A History* (Cassell, 1964 & 1969) with Roy Slater, *Racing An Historic Car* (M.R.P., 1960) and *The Vintage Alvis* (Macdonald, 1966) with Norman Johnson.

Film production Piagraph Limited
Ballantine Consultant Editor Prince Marshall
Foulis Production Editor Tim Parker